Last Rights

The Struggle over the Right to Die

Last Rights

The Struggle over the Right to Die

Sue Woodman

Plenum Trade • New York and London

Library of Congress Cataloging-in-Publication Data

Woodman, Sue.
    Last rights : the struggle over the right to die / Sue Woodman.
        p.   cm.
    Includes bibliographical references and index.
    ISBN 0-306-45995-7
    1. Right to die.   2. Assisted suicide.   I. Title.
    R726.W655   1998
    174'.24--dc21   98-28439
                                                                        CIP

ISBN 0-306-45995-7

©1998 Sue Woodman
Plenum Press is a Division of Plenum Publishing Corporation
233 Spring Street, New York, N.Y. 10013

http://www.plenum.com

10 9 8 7 6 5 4 3 2 1

Printed in the United States of America

Contents

Introduction

In the midst of writing this book, I received a call summoning me back to London, where I grew up, to the hospital bedside of my 90-year-old aunt. Aunty, as she is known to family and friends alike, had fractured her leg during a fall, and the physicians decided they would have to operate to reset the bone. This was the fourth time in 6 months that Aunty had been admitted to the hospital; the previous three times she'd needed treatment for her many chronic ailments: heart disease, high blood pressure, diabetes, arthritis, and pain caused by a badly fitted knee replacement. Now, because of this complicated medical history, combined with her advanced age, the physician in the orthopedic ward was calling me in New York (at the expense of the National Health Service, no less!) to warn me that fixing my aunt's fractured bone under anesthetic would be fraught with risk. She knew the risks and had agreed to the operation, he said, but as her next of kin, he felt I should be informed.

Because I am my aunt's closest relation—to all intents and purposes, her surrogate daughter, and the natural one to take responsibility for her in times of crisis—I felt I should be in London by her side. I figured that either she would survive the procedure, in which case she would be out of danger within a few days and I could go home, or she would not. If not, I would have to go back anyway to see to all of the business that attends the closing of a person's life. I had no idea that there might be another, even worse, outcome to the scenario.

When I arrived at the hospital the following morning, the physician told me that Aunty had survived the operation itself, but there was a problem. Perhaps related to her fracture, perhaps not, she had developed a blood clot in the broken leg, and no blood was reaching her toes or lower calf. The leg would have to be amputated some way above the knee. If not, he said, Aunty would die of gangrene, probably within a week.

The predicament was chilling and indigestible. I sat at her bedside; both of us were in a subdued state of shock.

I tried to encourage Aunty to talk, but she could not verbalize her inner turmoil. A Holocaust survivor who lost almost her entire family in the concentration camps, she had known so much pain that she has never found words for, so many horrors she has chosen not to talk about in her life. And now, at age 90, she had come on another horror. At one point, she wondered aloud what evil she had ever done to deserve such a cruel fate.

I asked her whether she was afraid to die. "No, no, I'm not afraid," she answered emphatically. "I would love it—just to go to sleep, to be finished. . . ." I tried to explain that this would be more or less possible: She could refuse the amputation, and allow her poor, battered, worn-out old body to die. The nursing staff promised they would make the process as easy and painless as possible; the morphine was already on order. Out of my love for her, I secretly prayed that she would choose this course of action.

Aunty belongs to a generation of women (I think it is women in particular) that holds physicians in enormously high esteem. She never questions their judgment. If they tell her to take a certain medicine, she'll take it, not really knowing what it is meant to do, other than "make her better." And even though her general health has deteriorated with age, she continued to believe, until the time of her fall, that some physician somewhere could administer a magic potion that would restore her once more to health, and even youth.

But now, suddenly, these godlike figures in white coats who came and went from her bedside with bewildering speed and variety, were asking *her* to make a decision, the decision of her life—and to make it virtually on the spot. Surprisingly, from the depth of her grief, she found words.

"If I have the surgery, what are my chances of surviving it?" Aunty asked the unsympathetic vascular surgeon, who clearly felt that such an old person shouldn't even bother to try. Yet he grudgingly put her odds at 50–50, maybe even 60–40. "Well, if I have a 50 percent or better chance, then obviously I'll have to take it," she said. And for her, the choice *was* obvious. Life, apparently, was worth the pursuit, even at such an enormous cost.

There was an amazing irony to all of this: Aunty had been miserable for years. Chronic illness, self-pity, and loneliness had robbed her of much pleasure in her life. During those last few months of futile hospital stays and declining health, Aunty had frequently expressed a wish to die. Yet now, confronted with the prospect, she was unwilling, or unable, to let go.

For a long time, both before the operation and afterwards, as the grim reality of her situation began to sink in, I questioned the wisdom of Aunty's choice. If she wasn't afraid of dying—if she even *wished* she were dead—then why had she chosen life? Life with such a long and arduous process of recovery stretching ahead? I posed this question to the physicians, the nurses, the night nurse who oversaw the few quiet hours that descend on the ward after midnight. All agreed that, in eight out of ten cases like hers, people choose to take their chance at survival, even when life ahead is likely to be challenging in the extreme, maybe even painful.

"So what *is* it that people fear, if they don't fear dying?" I persisted. Perhaps it was the manner of dying, they said: Aunty might understandably be afraid of a process that would cause her body to be slowly poisoned as toxins multiplied in her blood, but she might say yes to the bolt from the blue—a deadly dose of drugs, for example, or a lethal injection administered by a physician—that would carry her off painlessly and fast. Would her decision have been different if this option had been available?

To my surprise, very few of the medical professionals I talked to could accept the fact that, deep down, someone might not be afraid of death itself—that awesome, unknown chasm—however it came along. "Even if they say they're not afraid, I'm sure they are," said one young physician, obviously uncomfortable at finding himself in an impromptu philosophical debate. He hurried away; clearly, I thought, when it comes to death, physicians are just as uneasy with the subject as the rest of us—and probably just as afraid, if not more so. Since then, I've learned that most of them are also painfully ill-equipped to deal with dying patients. For the medical profession, death is a defeat—a frustration that they must work harder to prevent next time. It is virtually never regarded as a right, or even a desirable, outcome, the natural, inevitable conclusion to a life fully lived. And yet, in the current debate about physician aid in dying, it is our physicians whom we would look to to help us end our lives. While many are profoundly opposed to the concept of assisted death, there are a growing number who have come to believe that, for some patients whose pain and suffering cannot be controlled, hastening their dying is the most humane form of treatment their profession can offer.

Of course, even those who support the idea of physician-assisted dying do not expect the physician him- or herself to make the decision. Wouldn't it erode our trust in them if physicians were the ones to decide when to "give up" on our loved ones? I certainly didn't trust the imperious vascular surgeon who once a day swept through Aunty's ward, dispensing his medical judgments without emotion, seemingly oblivious to the fact that in those hospital beds, binding all of those damaged anatomical organs together, were human souls in search of solace as much as solutions. Had the decision over Aunty's fate been left up to that physician, I believe he would not have gone forward with the surgery. He would not have considered her worth saving, partly because of her age and frail health, partly to spare the beleaguered National Health Service the enormous cost of such a procedure and its aftermath.

In all honesty, I must add that if the decision had been left to me that day, I, too, would probably have decided not to proceed. In the shock of the moment, the idea of amputation seemed so brutal, so unbearable, that *I* couldn't face it. I feel sure that my reasoning was prompted by love of her, because I wanted to spare her the distress of coping with what lay ahead. But maybe on a deeper level my decision was also informed by self-interest. Being 3000 miles away from a needy relative—having to juggle the conflicting demands of her and my children—creates its own set of stresses. Perhaps my subconscious would have used the occasion to protest. In retrospect, I'm very happy I wasn't called on to decide.

Defying all of the odds, Aunty came through and two days later, she was sitting up in a chair, surrounded by flowers and messages from well-wishers. I sat with her, holding her hand. She was listless and depressed, unable to bring herself to raise the sheet to look at her heavily bandaged wound. She fretted over trivial details, unwilling to confront the real issues, such as whether she would ever get to go home again, or if she would now need to do what has always terrified her—move into an old age home. She dreaded what lay ahead. And so did I, knowing that I would soon have to return to New York and would be unable to help her in the long journey that lay ahead. Life seemed grim indeed.

But later that day, apropos of nothing, she said, "I think I made the right choice." What made her say that? Was it, perhaps, the sun streaming in through the windows, or an instant free of pain, a minuscule surge of well-being, that persuaded her, at least for that moment, that it was worth being alive? She may change her mind again when things get tough, as they surely will. But she may also agree, a year from now, that the company of her friends and the love of her family were worth the difficult journey back.

As for me, I received an instant but profound lesson in the infinite complexities of the "right-to-die" issue that is the subject of this book. I began to understand that each person's death is as different as his or her life, and that the decisions that surround any person's dying are likewise as delicate, and as individual. I realized how hard it is to be the judge of what, in the end, makes another's life worth living, or ending: It is so easy to undervalue the quality of a sick person's existence. Yet for those of us whose days on earth are increasingly finite, the line that defines what makes life worth-while is written in the sand.

As the daughter of a mother and father who, in different ways, survived the Holocaust, but who in collusion refused to talk about it, death has always been for me a terrifying and taboo subject. My dead relatives, killed in concentration camps at Auschwitz and Minsk, were constant shadowy presences in my childhood home: I knew something terrible had happened to them—grandparents, an aunt, an uncle, and even a 2-year old cousin—but no one would explain exactly what, and I quickly learned that I should not ask. I think my parents simply wanted to put the past behind them, and to protect the precious new generation they had produced from the unadulterated evil they had experienced in the world. But of course, their refusal to shine a light on that darkness only made it murkier and more menacing for me. And when my father died of cancer while I was still a teenager (they had hidden from us the first bout he had had when my sister and I were young children), and then a few years ago, when my mother had a heart attack and disappeared from our lives literally overnight, my sense of death as a terrifying, unnatural destroyer was only exacerbated.

But my aunt envies my mother her death, and after watching her struggles—as well as those of my contemporaries as they experience the difficult deaths of their parents—I certainly understand why. It is painful to watch our aging parents slow down and grow confused, agonizing to clean up their bodily messes, listen to their labored breathing, negotiate the suffering involved in their dying, and finally realize that one day, their suffering will be our own.

At one time or another we have all thought we would do anything—anything at all—to keep the people we love alive and with us forever. Yet many of us have come to learn that sometimes, death is preferable to life, and in the most extreme circumstances, as proof of our love, we would even choose to help those we love best to die.

Are we right to make that choice? And is it ours to make?

♦ **CHAPTER 1** ♦

The Twentieth-Century Battle over Death

If I must suffer without hope of relief,
I will depart, not through fear of the pain itself,
but because it prevents all for which I live.
—Seneca

Since the early 1990s, when the bizarre figure of Jack Kevorkian drove his now-famous rusty Volkswagen van onto the national scene, his front-seat passenger, death, has muscled its way into the headlines, into the nation's courtrooms and legislatures, and into our collective political consciousness. All of us, even those of us who are normally backseat drivers, have a stake in what is happening. For death, unlike other major social issues like abortion or capital punishment, concerns each of us. One by one, we are drawn into its thrall, first through the deaths of the people we love, then as we make our own mortal journeys.

For many, the inevitability of dying is too painful to contemplate. Our society is marked by a consummate denial of death; most of us prefer to pretend it doesn't exist. We shy away from making our wills and leaving instructions about the kind of end-of-life care we want. We fight the forces of nature to stay youthful, healthy, and, to the greatest degree possible, immortal. Our crusaders, the physicians, arm themselves with shiny modern machinery and powerful drugs to repel the enemy for as long as possible. Meanwhile, we remove the dying from the flow of everyday life and confine them to institutions. As recently as 50 years ago, the majority of people died at home. Today, 80 percent end their lives in hospitals and clinical care settings. And according to a very recent study on death and dying led by Dr. Joanne Lynn, director of the Center to Improve Care of the Dying at George Washington University School of Medicine in Washington, D.C., (published in *Annals of Internal Medicine,* January 1997), most of those people end their days in pain, breathlessness, depression, and confusion. Many patients are subjected to at least one form of "heroic" treatment before they die—cardiopulmonary resuscitation, or attachment to a respirator or a feeding tube—even though fully 59 percent of the patients in the study said they wanted comfort care rather than aggressive treatment in their final days of life.

As the first study to have been carried out on dying hospital patients in almost a century, Lynn's important research highlights two critical factors. First, we as a society have turned our back on death for too long. "Our cultural inclination," Lynn says, "is to disavow dying." Second, the study illuminates how stubborn physicians are in their determination to keep death at bay—even when the patients themselves make it clear that they don't want life-prolonging procedures.

Consequently, it is not surprising that so many of us fear being rushed into an intensive care ward, placed on life-support equipment, and made to linger in a state of semiexistence against our will. This particular fear seems to have grown in direct proportion to our physicians' abilities to perform these life-prolonging feats. The very measures that we once viewed as miracles of modern medicine can now be seen in a more critical light: Now we know that machines designed to prolong life can sometimes do nothing more than prolong the dying process. Many who once considered death too unpalatable to contemplate are beginning to realize that living can be worse than dying. As a result, more and more suffering people are asking their physicians to help them die, not keep them alive.

For these reasons, the right-to-die movement has emerged as an urgent social concern for the next century. It is the last frontier for personal choice or, as some regard it, the ultimate human rights crusade. The implementation of this "right" would cause a profound social revolution for the medical profession, the religious community, bioethicists, lawyers, philosophers, and, of course, for us, the patients and future patients, who would be able to invoke that "right" for ourselves. According to the proponents of assisted dying, now is the time for that revolution. As one advocate put it:

"We urgently need a modern set of ethics for a modern state of medicine."

The supporters of the right-to-die revolution are a variegated bunch: a loose coalition of physicians, lawyers, ethicists, and ordinary men and women, most of whom are united by their experiences with painful, protracted death. Their desire for a "good death"—a "death with dignity," as their inspirational mantra has it—is not simply an abstract concept or a worthy social principle. At the heart of almost every person's wish to take charge of his or her own death lies the story of a terrible end-of-life struggle of someone dear to them. Those who have witnessed a loved one lingering on to a desperate end, physically unable to let go of life—either because of medical intervention or the lack of it—have a particular determination not to meet the same fate themselves. That is why they joined one of the many right-to-die organizations such as the Hemlock Society, or Compassion in Dying, or are fighting to get the laws changed in their particular state. It is also why, as the movement has gained in momentum and respectability, they remain such dogged campaigners: As they say, the price of the status quo is just too high to pay.

Pitted against these campaigners are people who are just as fervent in their opposition: For them too, the stakes are high. Wresting control of death, they counter, represents metaphysical trespassing into God's domain, and it would seriously violate the integrity of the medical profession and its age-old oath to "do no harm." An increasingly vociferous group of opponents even fears that legalizing physician-assisted death could mark the beginning of society's moral descent toward a new kind of national eugenics program, in which the mentally and physically disabled would find themselves unwilling victims.

Are any of these fears justified? There is nothing new about people—with or without the involvement of their physicians—helping one another to end their lives when they are suffering without hope of relief. For centuries, these acts of mercy were carried out in the shadows, heavily guarded secrets kept locked within family or medical lore. No one knows how many people have died with another's help, or how many physicians have offered their patients this kind of assistance. But legal history is dotted with court cases involving physicians and loving family members who were tried and sometimes found guilty of charges from assisting death to murder. Most have been acquitted on compassionate grounds, but not all. As a result, families in search of physician assistance once had to turn to a kind of "underground railroad"—a network of people who contacted each other through coded messages, worked together secretly to perform what was necessary, and then never met or spoke of their actions again.

The new right-to-die movement has changed all of these rules. Finally, after decades of secrets and silence, both the dying and those who have helped the dying have started speaking out about meticulous plans, about stockpiling drugs, suffocating loved ones with pillows and plastic bags, administering carbon monoxide or increased doses of morphine. People have decided to tell their stories in the hope of shaking up what they see as archaic medical ethics, challenging religious doctrine, and changing outdated laws. In a remarkably short time, they have had great success around the world. At the time of this writing, physician-assisted dying has become legal in Colombia, was briefly legal in Western Australia (where supporters are fighting to reinstate it), and is widely practiced in certain parts of Europe, most notably the Netherlands. In the United States, proponents have managed to propel their cause onto the ballots and before the legislatures of several states. In October 1997, Oregon became the first U.S. state to make physician-assisted dying legal. Supporters have also tried to get assisted dying recognized as a constitutional right in two parts of the country—on the West Coast and in the Northeast—and in 1997, managed to gain a hearing before the Supreme Court. Although the Court refused to recognize the constitutionality of assisted dying, the judges readily acknowledged that the legal debate is in its infancy: There will undoubtedly be much more ahead.

The evolution of this movement is a textbook example of the growth of a modern social crusade. Its supporters have been helped by a fortuitous confluence of social factors: a growing population of elderly people, a health care system in a state of serious financial crisis, and an armamentarium of sophisticated medical technology whose use in end-of-life care is increasingly viewed with distrust. Right-to-die activists have applied modern political campaign techniques to their crusade. They have handpicked powerful and poignant human dramas to illustrate their position before the public and the courts; they have used skillful professionals as their spokespeople and, wherever possible, they have distanced themselves from perceived "extremists" such as Jack Kevorkian, America's best known, and most controversial, activist. They make efficient use of new technology by communicating with each other on the Internet and exchanging foolproof methods for "self-deliverance," including doses of drugs guaranteed to be lethal. In recent years, they have organized high-profile conferences, candlelit church vigils, and demonstrations on the steps of the U.S. Supreme Court. Lead players such as Kevorkian's lawyer, Geoffrey Fieger, and Hemlock Society founder Derek Humphry (handily, a former journalist) give interviews and press conferences with the media savvy of any well-seasoned political strategist. Indeed, today's right-to-die activists *are* political strategists, raising funds, drafting state initiatives, and increasing public awareness in their drive to change laws and influence national policy. A decade's worth of opinion polls shows that, with increased knowledge, public support for physician-assisted death has risen to, currently, around 70 percent. The level of support has never yet slipped.

Nevertheless, offering a hastily considered "yes" or "no" answer to a pollster does scant justice to the complex moral questions that entwine this particular subject, questions whose long-term ramifications have the power to shape our society well into the next century.

The largest question is whether the definition of a civilized society is one in which life is sacrosanct under all conditions, or one in which its people are free to determine their own fate, including its most fundamental prerogative—the freedom to cease to be. If we, as individuals, give ourselves that right, and begin to decide the measure of our lives—when we have had enough and when we want to leave it—how will we, as a society, be transformed by that right? Will we be transformed at all? And if we discover we have made a mistake, is there any way back, or will we find ourselves tumbling down a slippery slope, unable to stop the slide?

Profound human concerns are at stake in this debate, which is why we must all take part in it: we, the physicians, we, the lawmakers, and in particular, we, the human beings who will live—and die—according to the outcome. Whether we like it or not, the time for the debate is now. At the dawn of the twenty-first century, its momentum appears unstoppable.

CHAPTER 2

The Anguish of a
Difficult Death

A day less or more
At sea or ashore
We die—does it matter when?
—Alfred Lord Tennyson

For too many people, death comes, not as the peaceful con-clusion to a life, but as a violent and cruel destroyer. What it destroys, along with the life in question, is the possibility for release among those left behind. People say that for a long time afterwards, the memory of a painful death-struggle obliterates the much more precious images that they want to preserve. Whereas they wish to celebrate a life well-lived, they are left with haunting images of pain and suffering, of a once-vibrant person left too long in a horrible state of exis-tence that no longer resembled life.

In an era when ever fewer people experience the "death with dignity" that they hope for, more and more of them—pa-tients and their families alike—are growing desperate for a better way. Ordinary, law-abiding people, people who have led quiet, private lives and who always paid their parking fines, find themselves plotting an end to their loved ones' suffering, and in some cases, even taking responsibility for it. Sometimes, the difference between a natural death and a criminal act is simply a matter of time and endurance.

At the same time that Aunty was making her slow recuperation in a small room of a long-stay hospital, Elsie Martin was taking her time dying in the room next door. Elsie, 2 months away from her 90th birthday, had developed gangrene in her legs and had been told she needed to have both amputated, high up on the thigh. But after 4 years of deteriorating health related to heart disease, diabetes, and increasing blindness and deafness, she decided she wanted to die. No amputation, no more treatment, enough was enough. The physicians promised to keep her comfortable in her quiet, airy room, and estimated her dying would take 2 to 3 weeks.

Nine weeks later, Elsie was still hanging on, going in and out of consciousness, her gray, shriveled form lying silent on the pillow for 22 hours out of every 24. When she was awake, she would babble about her husband, dead for 18 years, and give the nurses lists of nonsensical chores to do. Still, members of Elsie's huge, devoted family—her 9 children, 29 grandchildren, and 50 great-grandchildren—took turns sitting by her bedside every day, their lives on hold as they waited for her to die.

As the family waited, the nurses were still doing everything possible to keep Elsie going: As well as giving her a steady flow of intravenous morphine to deaden her pain, they were also administering antibiotics and insulin, and feeding her—at least fluids.

"Why are they still doing all that, for God's sake?" her daughter said angrily one day. "Yesterday, we couldn't rouse her all day and I thought that she might have finally slipped into a coma. But then the nurse came in the evening and called her name over and over till she got her to wake, and then made her eat some soup. Why can't they just let her go? What do they think, that she'll ever get out of bed again?"

The point is, physicians and nurses can't bear to "let go": It goes against everything they are trained to believe. Death is the ultimate enemy, and their job is to fight it off—as hard and for as long as possible.

But is that always the right, the humane, thing to do? "I love my mother to pieces," her daughter says emotionally. "She's been the best mother in the world to us. But this isn't her, this bag of bones lying here, and this isn't how we want to remember her. Hasn't she gone through enough? If they want to help her, why can't they help her die?" Fighting back tears, she adds, "I never thought I'd ever pray for my mom to die, but I do. And I pray that others don't have to go through what we have, waiting and watching her like this. My husband said yesterday that we ought to put something in her soup. I know he was joking, only, well, you know. . . ."

Eventually, the hospital physician agreed to hold back medical treatment, yet the waiting went on for a full month longer. It's hard to believe Elsie's ancient ruin of a body could have held out that long. By the end, she no longer recognized her family, didn't even seem to be aware of whether they were there with her or not. But they were, dutifully and lovingly. I wonder what they were feeling when they left the hospital for the last time: grief, of course, but almost certainly great relief—for Elsie, and for themselves. And then possibly guilt for feeling relief. Death brings with it such complicated emotions.

Can we even imagine the profusion of emotions—guilt, grief, pain, relief, torment, fear, remorse, release—that people experience if their loved one's suffering becomes so severe that they feel finally driven to help that person die? It seems unimaginable. Yet for centuries, adoring mothers, devoted fathers, spouses, lovers, sons, and daughters have found themselves "unplugging" life-support systems, spoon-feeding fatal concoctions, stabbing, shooting, or smothering their loved ones, simply to end their agony. One 25-year-old man is currently serving a 40-year prison term for shooting his suffering mother; a Canadian father found guilty of killing his severely disabled 12-year-old daughter, is appealing his second-degree murder conviction. He simply couldn't bear to continue watching the child suffer, he said.

Is a mercy killing different from a murder? And what are we as a society if we don't recognize a distinction between the two, if we can't acknowledge the depths of people's love—and their despair?

Baptist Minister Henry Logan begged God for an end to his wife's unbearable suffering. He prayed every day, from the moment in 1995 when he realized that her cancer had spread and she would never get better. But as her disease advanced, her pain grew worse. So powerful was the experience of witnessing her agony that, in its aftermath, his life has taken a new direction: He is determined to help others find a better way of death.

Henry and his wife, Karen, lived a quiet, steady life in Lincoln, Nebraska, raising two children and working hard—he at his ministry and his charitable projects, she as a teacher at the local high school. The couple had been married for almost 30 years when she was diagnosed with multiple myeloma, a rare and deadly form of cancer that attacked her autoimmune system and her bones. An initial round of chemotherapy sent the cancer into remission for 3½ years, but then it returned, and Karen started losing ground. There was little the physicians could do to help her.

Toward what seemed to be the end of her life, Karen was hospitalized. Henry moved in to her hospital room to be with her. Her decline was catastrophic but, alas, painfully slow. She was in constant pain and would slip in and out of a drug-induced sleep—sometimes fitful, sometimes deep and heavy. One night when she awoke, she told her husband that she was tired of fighting, and simply wanted to die.

But 2 days later, Karen was still alive. She was on steady intravenous doses of morphine to try to control her unrelenting pain, yet she still couldn't find comfort or peace.

She decided to refuse food and water, as a way of speeding up her death. But still it wouldn't come. Then, as her lungs filled with fluid, Karen started gurgling with every breath she took. Henry found it unbearable to sit helplessly by her bedside and have to listen to the sound. At one point, he says, he snapped and tried to suffocate her with a martial arts hold. He crossed his wrists across her throat and pressed down. But as her face reddened and her body started flailing in resistance, he lost his nerve and retreated.

Sitting by her bedside through those endless days, Henry began feeling increasingly angry at his inability to help her. He was upset at the medical staff who were at once tender and painstaking in their care of Karen, but at the same time also arrogant and patronizing. Henry felt that the physicians had not been honest with them about the horror of Karen's dying, and he was furious that they did nothing to help put an end to it. Most of all, he felt anger at the Nebraska state legislature for failing to provide a legal option for people in Karen's position to end their life in a better way than she was doing. Henry vowed that if anything were to come out of Karen's gruesome suffering, it would be some amendment to that law. He pledged to do what he could about that.

I had arranged to talk with Henry Logan at a small hotel that would be convenient for him. He had willingly agreed to tell me about the final weeks of Karen's life, her agonizing disease and its effect on the family. We settled down in a pleasant, generically furnished room and talked for a long time, until late in the evening. I don't know whether he had originally planned to tell me all that he did, but in that anonymous setting, in the stillness of the hour, words began tumbling out and Henry made no move to stop them. Maybe it was a relief to let them go; I doubt that many others had heard them.

Henry told me that, after three endless and increasingly intolerable days of listening to his wife's labored breathing, he finally couldn't stand it anymore and decided to take action. Left alone in the room with her as she struggled on and on, he finally found a way to bring peace to his suffering wife.

"She was lying there, rasping and gurgling and almost suffocating, but never quite enough to end it," he recalled. He slipped the turban off her bald head (denuded by the ferocious chemotherapy drugs she had been taking) and pulled a plastic bag he had taken from the hospital supply room over her face.

"I sat on the bed and watched her breathing getting slower and slower, I saw the condensation form on the inside of the bag," he said. Finally, the gasping and rasping stopped. The room was silent. Karen was dead.

Henry removed the plastic bag, pushed it to the bottom of the trash can, and replaced Karen's turban. Then he kissed her and said his good-byes to her before opening the door to let the rest of the family know that she was finally at peace.

Was the deed hard to do? "It was demeaning and denigrating," Henry says. "The fact that it was a plastic bag—it conjures up a macabre, low-rent kind of thing, the associa-tion with a plastic bag being for trash, I suppose. And having to be secretive about it and to hurry—that was demeaning as well. I shouldn't have had to do it like that for someone I'd spent 35 years of my life with."

But Henry has no regrets about what he did, because he firmly believes he helped Karen escape her suffering. "It was an absolute necessity, as far as I'm concerned, and I'd have done the same thing even if it would have landed me in jail," he says. "Who better than me to help her? I ought to be the one who pays the price."

The price he is paying is something far removed from guilt, he insists. Yes, he agrees, it's a heavy load to carry, un-doubtedly a serious and traumatic deed to have done. But he sees it as part of the solemn obligation he had to the person with whom he had shared a life. "That's what life is—a time to be born and a time to die," he says. "It was an appropriate action within the context of our marriage."

What's more, Henry finds no ideological conflict between his religion and his having helped a loved one to die. And al-though Henry Logan is not his real name, he has sought anonymity in the telling of his story not for himself, but rather to protect his son and daughter, who are in high-pro-file professions and might be stigmatized by their father's act. He feels that for himself, both as a husband and as a minister, there is nothing for which he should be stigmatized.

"How can you be religious and *not* champion this point of view?" he said. "Must we live out the love of God in such a way that our loved ones must experience awful pain? Jesus was well known for standing against the law of the land. Must we be God's stewards and stand for God in all things except when it comes to the deathbed? Is that when we say, 'That's God's domain'?"

Today, Henry uses every opportunity he can to lobby for, and preach about, the need to change the laws relating to dying. He wants his beloved wife's death to stand for something. And he wants no one else, ever, to have to go through what he has gone through. That's what he prays for today.

Suffering comes in so many forms. Some, like Logan's, are about the need for action, and about living in the aftermath of difficult deeds done. For others, suffering is about inaction—the inability to do what they feel is needed, and the consequent pain of watching loved ones living out their lives in limbo—a physical or emotional no man's land.

Patients who have physical or mental conditions that are debilitating, unchanging, and with no end in sight cause grave concern for right-to-die activists on both sides, and raise some uncomfortable questions for society as a whole: What kind of "quality of life" do such patients really have, and who, if anyone, has a right to judge? What if there is no legally recognized health care proxy to represent the patient's wishes? And who decides when family members are divided about what they—and the muted patient—really want? These issues are all embodied in the harrowing story of the Martin family, from Moline, Michigan.

On January 16, 1987, Michael and Mary Martin, then both in their mid-30s, and their three children, Melinda, aged 11, Matthew, 5, and Melanie, 7, piled into their car and headed out to a local restaurant for dinner. Moments later, at an unlit and unfenced grade crossing near their home, their car was hit head-on by a train.

Rescue workers were on the scene within minutes. They found a horrifying scene of mangled steel, shattered glass, and blood. As they cut the Martins out of the wreckage of their car, they established the extent of the family's injuries. Mary had suffered multiple fractures and two collapsed lungs; Michael, who at first didn't appear too badly hurt, nonetheless was breathing strangely and had signs of broken bones and head injuries. Seven-year-old Melanie had been killed instantly. The surviving children were raced to local hospitals by ambulance. Mary and Martin were lifted into helicopters and flown to different trauma centers nearby.

In the grim aftermath of the crash, Mary made a painfully slow but eventually complete recovery. But Michael, found to be suffering from devastating brain injuries, was left partially paralyzed and totally incapacitated. He could not walk, talk, eat, or roll over in bed. He needed a feeding tube for food and water, and a catheter and a colostomy to perform basic functions. All he could do unaided was breathe, open his eyes and stare blankly, nod his head, and smile. Michael smiled fixedly: when the physician described to him the extent of his injuries; when he was told about Melanie's death; when he was asked whether he wanted to go on living. And he smiled when he was asked if he wanted to die.

"Mike had often talked to me about how he would never want to live in this kind of a state, and I promised him I would never let him," says Mary Martin. So 5 years after the accident, in 1992, after Mary had settled a lawsuit with the railroad company, she turned her attention to her husband's wishes. As his legal guardian, she approached the physicians, social workers, and bioethics committee at his hospital about the possibility of withdrawing his feeding tube. The hospital said that although the procedure would be medically appropriate, they would need legal authorization before they could proceed. Unaware of what she was getting into, Mary took Michael's case to court.

This was the beginning of a long and acrimonious journey through a legal system painfully ill-equipped to deal with modern-day medical nightmares. What made the Martin case especially complicated was that it was the first right-to-die case·in the United States involving someone who was not mentally competent, yet who was not in a coma or in a persistent vegetative state. The law is clear that in such cases, life-sustaining equipment, such as a respirator or (in this case) a feeding tube, can lawfully be removed when the guardian believes that is what the patient would want. But no one knew how to rule in a case where the patient was sitting up and smiling, yet was unable to make his wishes known.

Mary, who said she and Michael had discussed the matter a number of times over the years, insisted she knew what his wishes were. But then so did Michael's sister, Patricia Major, and his mother, Leeta Martin. They both insisted that Michael didn't want to die.

"I believe Michael wants to live. I think if he didn't, he'd have died the night of the accident," Major said in court. "Michael told me he wouldn't want to live on a respirator, in a coma. Well, he's not. Michael's happy. He has accepted what his life is now."

In the tense atmosphere of the Michigan courtroom, Major and Leeta Martin accused Mary of dark ulterior motives. She wanted him dead, they claimed, because she was after his money. They also accused Mary of wanting to be free to marry a man with whom she had recently become involved. Mary answered that she had no intention of that; she was quite content with the way things were. And as for the money, she'd received a sizable compensation of her own from her settlement with the railroad, larger than Michael's, so why would she be after more? She also pointed out that since Michael would receive his compensation only for so long as he was alive, she actually would be worse off as his widow than as his wife.

The heavyweight family bout went four entire rounds. Patricia Major and Leeta Martin found that they had attracted a considerable cheering section of disabled rights and right-to-life activists who felt that the quest to end Michael's life posed a threat to the safety of all disabled people everywhere. Mary said that she had no hidden agenda, no wish to threaten anyone else—she merely wanted to fulfill her husband's wishes.

At the first hearing before a local court, Mary Martin's request to remove Michael's feeding tube was denied. The judge ruled that Michael had left no written proof—no 'clear and convicing evidence'—of his wishes. But the Michigan Court of Appeals decided to reverse the lower court and to grant Mary her request. Her opponents took the case back into court, and this time, the local judge reversed himself and decided in favor of Mary: Despite his personal beliefs in the right to life, he said, he considered Mary to be acting "with only Michael's interests in mind." But back in the Court of Appeals once again, the superior judges also changed their minds, ruling, for the fourth and last time, that Michael's feeding tube could not be removed—and their word was final. Mary Martin had exhausted all of the legal moves. As the very last blow, the U.S. Supreme Court declined to hear the case. There was nowhere else for her to go.

Today, more than a decade later, the Martins' case is still unresolved. Michael's condition remains unchanged, and Mary remains powerless to take any further action. Not even a change in legislation in favor of physician-aided dying would help her in her quest, for Michael is neither terminally ill nor competent to make his own wishes known—conditions that will almost certainly accompany any right to die granted by the law. Yet, because he's technically conscious, Michael is also unable to benefit from the existing law that enables a person in a coma or a persistent vegetative state to be "un-plugged" from his or her feeding tube. He seems condemned to exist in a state of legal, as well as mortal, limbo.

During the decade that has passed since the accident, the Martins' surviving daughter, Melinda, now 22, has had two children and their son, Matthew, is an athletic 16-year-old who plays soccer and is learning to drive. Mary has moved in with the man she met after the accident, and is now helping him raise his son. "I had to get on with my life," she says. But her sense of responsibility to her husband remains strong, and she still hasn't given up searching for ways to end Michael's ordeal. She is currently exploring whether she could be accused of murder if Michael's feeding tube became disconnected—as it often does of its own accord—and she failed to alert the nursing staff to have it put back in. She still hopes that the time will come when she can honor his wish to be allowed to die—however long the fight might take her. "I promised him," she repeats. "I feel I can't let him down."

Meanwhile, Michael sits in his nursing home and smiles.

CHAPTER 3

"Death with Dignity"
The Hope of a Movement

Sometimes death is a small victory.
—Chinese proverb

Like Tolstoy's vision of happy marriages, good deaths are, in our imaginings, all alike: peaceful and painless, occurring in a familiar bed at a hearty old age, and surrounded by loved ones. In real life, very few deaths are like that: In two out of three cases, for people like Elsie Martin and Karen Logan, they are painful, prolonged, and, more often than not, orchestrated by medical technology, not by nature.

Given this statistic, some of us might feel lucky just to be spared life-sustaining equipment or heavy sedation. We might even redefine a good death as one involving the help of a sympathetic physician and a handful of drugs: a quick and painless way of ending all suffering, while retaining some sense of personal dignity and control.

death in our own hands a blessing

For many years, Sandra Wiener described her desired death in those terms: She was desperate not to end up unceremoniously attached to tubes or machines, and she wanted a physician to help her make a quick, painfree exit from the world. When the time came, she was lucky enough to die exactly as she had wanted.

Yet it wasn't easy. As recently as 1990, which was when 64-year-old Sandra began to prepare for her death, assisted dying was an unmentionable, intensely private procedure. The steps she had to take to get a physician to prescribe a lethal dose of drugs were furtive and top secret. No one but her physician knew what she was planning, and they spoke together in veiled, hushed language, forging between them a crude shorthand, a virtual code.

In 1996, just six years after Sandra's death, her only daughter, Katherine, stands clutching a glass of wine at an elegant Park Avenue cocktail party, watching the celebrities of the right-to-die movement gathered together over canapés, discussing what will happen if the Supreme Court declares assisted death a Constitutional right, and the work that needs to be done in preparation. Here are the founders of organizations that for years had sent her mother right-to-die literature under plain, unidentified wrappers. Here, a philosophy that Katherine and her mother could only whisper about when they were alone is being openly and enthusiastically promoted. Katherine marvels at how much the climate has changed, and how fast.

"We were so alone with this at the time—it felt as if we were the only ones in the world to be going through what we did," she says. "And now . . . well, my mother would be smiling to see this."

Sandra Wiener, a dynamic and respected New York psychotherapist, was diagnosed with breast cancer in 1978 and underwent a radical mastectomy and a difficult round of chemotherapy. She felt horrible and lost her hair and eventually decided that traditional medicine was not for her. Instead, she chose a rigorous course of alternative treatment based on vitamin and mineral supplements and a carefully monitored nutritional plan. Her cancer went into remission, and she enjoyed 9 disease-free years of good health and energy. But in 1987, her physician discovered that the cancer had metastasized to Sandra's lungs and bones. The prognosis was not good.

Although she decided to keep the news a secret from all of her friends, her husband and daughter knew the truth. And, according to Katherine, they knew what Sandra would want to do.

"During all the good years, she'd been unwavering in her clear commitment that she didn't want to die a cancer death in a hospital, stuck with tubes and wearing adult diapers," Katherine says. She wanted to die at home, in her own way. Katherine promised she would do what was needed to help her.

Sandra approached her general practitioner. Through a series of indirect conversations about "friends" and "hypothetical situations," using phrases such as "just out of interest" and "let's suppose," she made it clear to her physician that she wanted to die before her disease made her dependent on others for her care, and she wanted the physician to help her. And in the same manner, her physician let her know that he was willing. He handed her a prescription for two drugs—Seconal and phenobarbital—enough of each to make a deadly dose. Later, he called Sandra at home to remind her—hypothetically of course—that before swallowing a lot of medicine, it is always a good idea to take some Maalox—to ensure that the pills will remain in the stomach, and not be vomited back up.

Sandra kept her supply of drugs untouched at home for several months while she planned when and how she would take them. Her cancer had by then spread to her hip, and as her bones disintegrated, she was in considerable and growing discomfort. But she refused surgery and hobbled around with the use of a cane, lying to friends about the reason, hiding her disease from her patients. No one seemed to suspect a thing. But Sandra knew that the end was coming, and she continued making her plans.

At first, she refused to discuss any details with Katherine; she told her she didn't want anyone else involved, that she didn't want to incriminate anyone by her actions. But when Katherine begged to be included, and stressed how much she wanted to be there when it happened, her mother relented: They would be in this thing together, as they had been throughout the disease.

In early 1990, when a tumor began to grow in Sandra's throat, obstructing her esophagus, she realized that, to be able to swallow her potion, she would have to act soon. She chose a day, 1 week away, and said that would be the time. Katherine, who had lived with this impending moment for so long, steeled herself for the event.

It was a cool spring evening when Katherine made her way over to visit her mother for what she knew would be the last time. She felt a heaviness, but also a steady resolve. She knew her mother's health was now fading fast and that if the moment were lost, she would probably end up as she had always feared—with a feeding tube in her stomach, and wearing a diaper. She knew that for her proud and headstrong parent, that would be a fate worse than death.

Katherine arrived at the apartment to find Sandra in bed, weak in body, but unshakable in her determination. She would die, as she had decided, later on that evening. Yet she procrastinated until two in the morning, still wanting to talk, noticing little details for the first time; for example, that there was a piece of tape stuck to the television cable box, and she wondered how she had managed to miss it until now.

Finally, Sandra asked Katherine for some paper and a pen. Weak as she was, she wrote a letter in an unwavering hand, to be given to her friends after her death.

As her mother wrote, Katherine went into the kitchen to make her some tea. She emptied the drugs into the cup, stirred well, and brought it to her mother.

"She only drank a little of the tea, and then she asked me to leave the room," Katherine recalls. "When I went back in, she was already unconscious and breathing in a deep, rattling way. She was still holding the cup. And there was a tear on her cheek."

Sandra had made her daughter promise not to try to resuscitate her. "That was the scariest thing: I didn't know if I would have to watch her die of a horrible reaction, or, as was my worst fear, whether she would aspirate. In the end, she didn't do any of the things I feared. She just slipped away. It all went very smoothly, exactly as she'd wanted it. I saw that as a gift from God."

Sandra took her last, faint breath at around 4 AM. To achieve the death she had wanted, two crimes had been committed: one by the physician who prescribed the drugs, and the other by Katherine, who had prepared the fatal mixture for her mother.

Early the next morning, Sandra's physician came to the apartment and nervously called the coroner to report the death. Would this be the moment of truth? He was relieved to discover that when a terminally ill person under the care of a physician dies at home, there is no call for an autopsy. The physician wrote on her death certificate that the cause of death was terminal cancer.

Despite knowing that she has committed a felony, Katherine carries her mother's death with her daily as a source of peace and deep satisfaction. "I wanted her to fight, and she did fight, and she survived for a long time—12 years—longer than all the other cancer patients in her support group," Katherine says. "And I wanted her to have the good death that she so desperately wanted, and she had that too. Caring for my mother was my life for a very long time," she adds. "I know that she got what she wanted, and what she did to get it was 100 percent the right thing to do."

Sandra Weiner left her own mark of approval on her death. When her shocked friends were told the news, they were also given her farewell letter. For them, and for the many other people who have read it since, most of whom have never met its author, the letter has become a testament to the power of choosing a dignified and peaceful death—at home, without pain, and without the life-protracting interference of futile medical intervention.

"I began to believe that my 3 year valiant fight was coming to a close—And you know what?—Instead of sadness, I felt peace," Sandra wrote of her final weeks of life.

I began to see that although the mind and emotions want more life—the body has a way of teaching us that it quite logically gets finished—and that it's O.K. I am sure some people would have dashed into the hospital for the latest combo of chemotherapeutic drugs with their very small success rate. But I felt well. I wanted to go peacefully feeling well—living my life on my terms to the end. Not dying in a hospital, sick and emaciated on god-forbid a series of tubes and a respirator. . . .

Anyway, I made my choices. I had superb medical physicians. I was loved and cared for. I have no regrets. I think I got as much mileage out of this body as I could have expected.

Yet it is not my wish to leave all of you so soon. But I got a great deal out of the years I spent with each of you. I am peaceful and have no fear. I wish you all the best and thank you for being my nearest and dearest.

Please celebrate my life. My home is open to you for three nights following my death.

I will probably be there in some form saying sit here—eat something and 'I love you'.

CHAPTER 4

The Right to Die
An Argument as Old as Life Itself?

Man is the only creature who knows that he will die.
                                        —Voltaire

For as long as people have been dying, societies have held opinions as to the value of their deaths: whether they are noble and transformational, or cowardly and sinful, even treasonous. Over the centuries, these judgments have shifted along with the ethical values of the age. No kind of death has elicited such dramatically changing convictions as death by suicide and assisted suicide.

The first evidence of a tolerance for suicide and voluntary euthanasia comes from ancient Greece. This era held some taboos about taking life: Aristotle said, "To kill oneself to escape from love or poverty or anything else that is distressing is not courageous" (*The Ethics of Aristotle*). But for the Greeks, there was nothing blameworthy about choosing to stop suffering at the end of life; sometimes, they believed, it was a worthy and sensible choice. The writer Plutarch said that in Sparta, infanticide was practiced on children who lacked "health and vigor." And Socrates, according to Plato, announced that painful disease and suffering were perfectly acceptable reasons to choose to end one's life: "Eu" (good) and "thánatos" (death)—the words that have given us "euthanasia"—was the desired end to a life well lived.

The Stoics, also, approved of suicide when it was used to end a life that had fallen out of harmony with nature. The best known of the Stoics, Seneca, who praised suicide as the last act of a free man, wrote prolifically about death in *Epistulae Morales*:

> It makes a great deal of difference whether a man is lengthening his life or his death. But if the body is useless for service, why should one not free the struggling soul? Perhaps one ought to do this a little before the debt is due, lest, when it falls due, he may be unable to perform the act.

In time, attitudes would change dramatically. With the rise of the Judeo-Christian religions in the second and third centuries, euthanasia came to be seen as either suicide or murder—both of which were morally abhorrent and sinful. Christianity, Judaism, and Islam all condemned euthanasia and held that human life was sacred. Christians in particular warned of the toll such a death would take on the immortal soul, and those who committed suicide were denied a Christian burial. In the thirteenth century, St. Thomas Aquinas pronounced suicide to be the most dangerous of all sins because it violated the sixth commandment, and allowed the dying person no time for true repentance.

But the dawn of the Renaissance in the fourteenth century brought yet another change of view. With their admiration of classical Greco-Roman values, people reevaluated suicide as a reasonable option. In 1516, in *Utopia,* his depiction of an idealized world, Sir Thomas More wrote:

> Since your life's a misery to you, why hesitate to die? You're imprisoned in a torture chamber—why don't you break out and escape to a better world. . . . We'll arrange for your release. . . . If the patient finds these arrangements convincing, he either starves himself to death, or is given a soporific and put painlessly out of his misery. But this is strictly voluntary.

This tolerance of suicide, and the respect for the right of individuals to choose how they died, lasted through the eighteenth century. Essayists and philosophers wrote longingly of death. John Donne, in his celebrated muse, Biothanatos, argued for the right to suicide as a form of voluntary euthanasia.

By the end of the nineteenth century, and into the twentieth, professionals and intellectuals (including Karl Marx) began serious study of the issues involved in euthanasia. In Britain, attempts were made to advocate its legalization. The Voluntary Euthanasia Society, formed in 1935, was the first organization of its kind in the world. Early members included the novelist H. G. Wells and Lord Listowel, an aristocrat and activist who remained a member of the society for 51 years, until he resigned in 1996. In 1936, the first of 3 attempts was made to introduce a law endorsing voluntary euthanasia in the British parliament. It failed by a margin of 35 to 14. One of the Royal Physicians, Lord Dawson of Penn, argued that legalizing the practice wasn't necessary as good physicians already helped their patients to die. History has shown that the physician was speaking from personal experience: Earlier that year, he had hastened the death of King George V with a combination of morphine and cocaine.

The darkest time in the history of euthanasia was undoubtedly the German eugenics program of the 1920s and 1930s. With government approval, the new Social Democratic party elected euthanasia committees and began a program of annihilating those with "Lebensunwerte Leben"—lives unworthy of living. Those deemed to be unworthy of life included anyone who was found to be a burden on the state: the physically handicapped, the mentally retarded, people too weak to care for themselves. The Germans coined another term for them, "unnütze Esser"—useless eater. Within a 2-year period, between 1939 and 1941, the authorities had killed 100,000 of their own citizens. They were Aryan Germans—none of them even Jewish.

The true facts of the German eugenics program only came to light after the war was over, at the 1946 Nuremberg War Crimes Trials. And more is coming to light, even to this day. As recently as 1996, evidence was emerging of the role that Austrian physicians had played in selecting children for scientific experiments. Like their German neighbors, uncounted hundreds were put to death in the name of science. Four hundred brains of children and teenagers, carefully labeled and preserved in formaldehyde, still survive in one of the country's leading psychiatric clinics, Am Steinhof, in Vienna.

The horror of the Nazi acts has cast a long pall over the rest of this century, and for many years after World War II, almost no one dared to advance the idea of euthanasia. As Humphry and Wickett suggest in *The Right to Die,* the Germans tarnished the meaning of "euthanasia" as "the good death"—perhaps forever.

The desire for assisted dying, however, did not diminish. In fact, it increased sharply as medical technology grew more sophisticated, through the 1960s and 1970s. Although it is hard to pinpoint the exact start of a social movement, the date generally cited for the birth of the modern right-to-die movement is March 31, 1976, the day when the New Jersey Supreme Court allowed the parents of a comatose young woman to take her off a life-support machine.

That young woman, Karen Ann Quinlan, quickly became a symbol of the new crusade. Because of her heartbreaking physical state and the measures taken to keep her alive, Quinlan's case jolted people into rethinking the so-called miracles that modern medicine was providing. As the American people were fed minute details of the Quinlan family's legal fight, they found themselves considering the circumstances for themselves. What would they want for their own daughter if she lay comatose in a hospital, kept alive by a machine? And if they'd want the machine switched off, how could they avoid going through the torturous legal process that the Quinlans endured to guarantee that they'd get their wish?

Karen Ann Quinlan was just 21 years old when she collapsed at a party and was taken to St. Clair's Hospital in Denville, New Jersey. No one is sure exactly what happened to her, but it is thought that a combination of Valium and alcohol depressed her metabolism and caused her breathing to stop twice—for 15 minutes or longer at a time. By the time paramedics brought her to the hospital, she was found to be in a persistent vegetative state, beyond hope of recovery.

Quinlan was kept alive for a few months by means of a respirator and a food tube into her stomach. After consulting a Catholic priest, her devoutly religious parents decided they wanted no more "extraordinary measures" taken to keep their daughter alive. They asked the hospital to pull the plug on her respirator. But the hospital refused, citing the "do no harm" stricture of the Hippocratic oath, and most of Quinlan's nurses, who were Catholic themselves, also refused to cooperate. The Quinlans took their case to court.

In court, the judge sided with the parents and ordered the hospital to unhook Quinlan's breathing apparatus. Yet because the nurses had carefully weaned her off it in anticipation of the judge's decision, Quinlan managed to breathe on her own. She survived another 9 years, kept alive through a nutrition and hydration tube, never regaining consciousness. By the time she died, in June 1985, she weighed 65 pounds and had spent the last years of her life curled in a fetal position. She finally succumbed to acute pneumonia, which, according to the wishes of her family, was left untreated.

Quinlan's eventual death must have seemed like an empty victory for the devoted parents who, for almost a decade, had regularly driven the almost 40-mile journey to and from the hospital to visit their comatose daughter. But for America, the court case that Karen Ann Quinlan inspired became a historic stepping stone to the future.

The most important aspect of the Quinlan case was the decision by New Jersey's Supreme Court that the patient's right to privacy was broad enough to include the decision to forego life-sustaining medical treatment. The court also ruled that because Quinlan was comatose, and therefore unable to decide her own fate, her father, who had brought the petition to court, could make the decision for her. What's more, as James M. Hoefler notes in *Deathright: Culture, Medicine, Politics, and the Right to Die,* this was the first time in a major right-to-die case in which "the court freely interjected itself into the sacrosanct physician–patient relationship as an arbiter of rights and wrongs."

The Quinlan case had further ramifications: It made Americans take action. In its aftermath, more than one and a quarter million people approached the Euthanasia Education Society for copies of their model living will, a document designed to instruct medical staff about patients' wishes for treatment—or the lack of it—if the patients could no longer communicate themselves.

Lawmakers also took up the cause. In 38 states across the country, they introduced legislation to deal with perceived inadequacies in their end-of-life procedures. By 1977, eight states—California, New Mexico, Arkansas, Nevada, Idaho, Oregon, North Carolina, and Texas—had signed right-to-die bills into law. California also introduced the Natural Death Act, which was the first piece of legislation to recognize the legitimacy of living wills. Today, 46 states honor living wills as legally binding documents that specify a patient's wishes for end-of-life care.

Despite this flurry of legal activity, the day-to-day work of physicians and hospitals remained almost unaffected. Physician aid in dying remained an issue that generated little heat, until one man sensed its social potential, and decided to take up the banner for the cause.

In 1978, Derek Humphry, a British journalist, published *Jean's Way,* a moving account of his wife, suffering as a result of terminal cancer, and his own role in helping her to die. The confession was explosive, bringing an outpouring of compassion from readers and enormous media interest in a subject that till that point had been virtually taboo. After the book's publication, Humphry spent several months waiting to hear whether the British Director of Public Prosecutions would indict him for his role in her death—an indictment that could lead to a 14-year prison term. The DPP, possibly swayed by all of the sympathy the story had evoked, decided to drop the case. By then, Humphry had remarried an American woman named Ann Wickett, and settled in California.

In 1980, Humphry and Wickett formed the National Hemlock Society. Its aims were to "support the option of active voluntary euthanasia for the terminally ill" under certain conditions: that the final decision to terminate life should be the patient's; and that the patient be genuinely terminal, not depressed or traumatized, or driven by financial considerations. The people who attended the first meeting were reluctant to put their name to such a concept, so great was the stigma around their stated purpose. By this time there had been euthanasia societies in existence in the United States since the late 1930s—notably the Euthanasia Education Council and the Society for the Right to Die, both modeled after the British Voluntary Euthanasia Society. But the activities and political intentions of those organizations concentrated on educational and philosophical questions of death and the enacting of state legislation, and were timid in comparison with those of the new Hemlock Society. Hemlock had more radical objectives in mind, such as helping sick people achieve their end-of-life objectives. It was also the only organization that invited people to join and participate. Eventually, enough charter members did sign on, and the first activist euthanasia society was in business.

Although the Hemlock Society grew only slowly through the 1980s (small chapters were formed in a number of cities), there was a significant jump in the numbers of so-called mercy killings and double suicides in those years. In his 1989 history of the movement, "The Right to Die: An Historical and Legal Perspective of Euthanasia," Humphry notes that slightly more than half of the mercy killings since 1920 took place in the 1980s, a quarter of them in 1985 alone—a 300 percent rise from any prior year.

Sociologists have speculated about the reasons for this jump, but have not come up with definitive answers. Some suspect that it may have been the changing atmosphere around the right-to-die question; others guess that it was because information on how to die was seeping into the public arena. Humphry himself had put some of it out there with his 1981 book, *Let Me Die Before I Wake,* America's first guide to what he called "self-deliverance," which included suicide methods and correct drug dosages woven as discreetly as possible into a succession of true stories. To begin with, copies of the book were made available only to Hemlock members.

By the early 1990s, the growing interest in the right to die movement became apparent in public opinion surveys. These showed that more than half of the American public was now in favor of physician-assisted death and membership of the Hemlock Society rose dramatically to reach 50,000. (Today, there are approximately half that number of members. Executives say this is not due to any lessening of support for the issue, but rather to the proliferation of right-to-die groups across the country, and the numerous separate state initiatives into which advocates have directed their energies.) With increased public interest, the stage was set for an explosive swell of activity: in the courts, in professional medical journals and institutions, and, most significantly, in the homes of the American people.

The decade began with a development that overnight transformed the face of the right-to-die debate. A retired pathologist, Dr. Jack Kevorkian, helped a 54-year-old woman suffering from the early stages of Alzheimer's disease to end her life. The event drew attention to patients' desperate desire for a physician's help in ending their suffering. Luckily for Kevorkian, he happened to live and operate in Michigan, a state with no coherent laws banning assisted suicide, and despite four separate attempts to prosecute him, he has been acquitted of wrongdoing on each occasion. To date, Kevorkian has admitted having assisted in more than 100 patients' deaths. He vows to continue doing so, undeterred, until his own death.

At the same time as Kevorkian was out challenging society in the streets, a handful of legal decisions being made in the courts was also chipping away at the topography of assisted dying. The most important decision was *Cruzan v. Director, Missouri Department of Health,* which became the first right-to-die case to reach the U.S. Supreme Court, and the one that established the right of comatose patients to be taken off life support.

The case involved a 26-year-old Missouri woman named Nancy Cruzan, who was horribly injured in a car accident in 1983. The physicians were unable to revive her, and she was placed in a state-run health care facility, where she spent 4 years in a coma. She could breathe on her own but had to be nourished by means of a feeding tube that was surgically inserted in her stomach.

At the end of those 4 years, Cruzan's parents had come to terms with the fact that Nancy was in a persistent vegetative state from which she would never recover. They requested that Nancy have her feeding tube removed. When the nursing home refused, for fear of being charged with murder, the family took their case to court. The judge accepted that as Nancy's guardians, the Cruzans had the right to act for her, and approved their request to stop artificial feeding. He also agreed with them that there was evidence that Nancy would not want to continue that way.

But, reluctant to stop treatment, the Missouri Department of Health challenged the case in their state supreme court. By a vote of 4 to 3, the judges decided that the evidence her parents had presented about Nancy's wish not to live in a vegetative state was unreliable. They also decided that because the young woman was neither brain dead nor terminally ill, she should be kept alive.

By the time the Missouri Supreme Court had reached this conclusion, in November 1988, the U.S. Supreme Court had already decided that it wanted to hear the case, to make its own judgment about the constitutional rights of a patient in Nancy's position to have treatment withdrawn. It was to be an important and historic case.

It was a case that, technically, the Cruzan family lost. The justices' majority opinion, announced in June 1990, affirmed that Nancy had the right to refuse unwanted medical treatment. But they did not make specific reference to the feeding tube, nor did they label her right a "fundamental liberty." Rather, they returned the case to the Missouri courts for a final decision, which should be based, they said, on whether Nancy had left sufficient "clear and convincing evidence" that discontinuing treatment was what she really would have wanted. In early December 1990, on the strength of testimony from several of her friends, the Missouri judge acknowledged that "clear and convincing evidence" existed and finally allowed the family to turn off Nancy's feeding tube. On December 26, twelve days after the tube was removed, and 8 years after her terrible accident, Nancy Cruzan died.

With the Cruzan case, the court established two important principles that, in the ensuing years, have come to be applied to hundreds of right-to-die cases nationwide: First, that within common law, people have the right to refuse treatment, even if that refusal may lead to their death. Second, it established that there *are* constitutionally protected rights involved in cases like Nancy's—specifically, the right to liberty that is guaranteed by the Fourteenth Amendment, which includes the right to avoid unwanted medical treatment. Furthermore, the court voted to uphold Missouri's insistence that there must be "clear and convincing evidence" of a patient's wishes. This remains a requirement in several states when a family member or friend appeals to suspend treatment on behalf of a comatose or vegetative patient.

The Cruzan case deeply affected many people who followed it, among them Missouri Senator John Danforth. Danforth, who before becoming a senator was a Protestant minister, was so appalled by Nancy's fate that he introduced into Congress the Patient Self-Determination Act, which became law in December 1991. The Act states that all hospitals, nursing homes, health care facilities, and HMOs must give their Medicare and Medicaid patients information on their health care rights, enabling them to make living wills and powers of attorney, and to decide in advance whether to accept or refuse life-sustaining treatments. The Patient Self-Determination Act was the first federal law that held a patient's wishes to be above those of the physician or the medical institution.

Many physicians were in total agreement with this move to give patients an increased say in their treatment. In his own way, a 42-year-old New York physician, Timothy Quill, was after the same result when he published his revolutionary article, "Death and Dignity: A Case of Individualized Decision Making," in the *New England Journal of Medicine* in March 1991. In the article, Quill admitted that he had given a terminally ill patient, only identified as "Diane," the wherewithal to end her life. By going public with this confession, Quill, a primary care physician at the University of Rochester School of Medicine, risked both his professional and personal freedom. He also threw down a gauntlet to his fellow physicians—a gauntlet that has continued to lie discomfitingly at their feet.

Was Quill wrong to accept—as Diane did—that there was no cure for her fatal form of leukemia, and that she had the right to reject medical intervention and to be helped to die? Or was society wrong to insist that as her physician, Quill could not help her have a peaceful passing, and instead had to allow her to face her death alone, without her physician or her loved ones present at the end?

Quill's admission of complicity in Diane's death caused a media frenzy as reporters sought out, and discovered, the true identity of the dead woman, and waited to hear whether Quill would be prosecuted for his role in her death. In the end, no charges were brought. But the experience transformed Quill into a passionate reformer, a physician who believes that helping his patients die well is as important a part of his work as helping them live well.

The same year that Quill's article appeared, Derek Humphry wrote another book that would become a publishing legend, and also shine more light on the shady subject of assisted death. *Final Exit,* a more specific version of the earlier *Let Me Die Before I Wake,* dispensed with personal stories and instead forthrightly listed drugs and the dosages needed to make them lethal. The book began life on the Hemlock Society's printing press, as a manuscript that could not find a commercial publisher. But, in the jargon of the industry, the book had great word of mouth. Apparently, America was hungry for a how-to manual for death, a book that would address honestly the concerns that many had about dying painfully and protractedly, and that would show them ways to avoid such an end. Readers pored greedily over the book's large, easy-to-read typeface, and learned from it not only which drugs to take, in what quantities, but also the "backup" method of using a plastic bag to ensure that there would be no chance of survival. The plastic bag, although widely condemned for its crudeness, has become a trademark Hemlock Society procedure.

Although *Final Exit* was assailed for potentially providing information to inappropriate groups, like troubled adolescents or those suffering from depression, it became a national bestseller. It sold half a million copies and remained on the *New York Times* bestseller list for 18 weeks.

The final important event of 1991 was the appearance on the state of Washington's ballot of the very first initiative to legalize physician aid in dying. Initiative 119 proposed minor revisions to the existing state law that would recognize physicians' rights in helping a terminal patient to die. The initiative was defeated by a margin of 56 percent to 44. But given the narrowness of the vote for this first-time issue, activists took heart and pledged to fight on. Up and down the West Coast, right-to-die advocates continued to explore ways of making physician aid in dying legal. By 1992, Californians had drawn up Proposition 161, a bill sanctioning physicians to prescribe lethal injections and drugs to patients, to help them end their lives. This proposition was also rejected, by 54 to 46 percent.

But 3 years later in Oregon, Measure 16, a law permitting physicians to prescribe potentially deadly drugs to their terminally ill patients, was finally voted into law, by the slimmest of margins: 51 percent to 49. Not only was the Death with Dignity Act the country's first right-to-die statute, but Oregon was the first place in the world where such a law had come into force, not through the efforts of legislators or justices, but rather through the will of the populace itself.

Not surprisingly, the initiative was challenged immediately. Opponents claimed it was unconstitutional and sent it back into the legal limbo of the appeals court. It took a full 3 years for the state's supreme court to declare that the measure was indeed legitimate, and should be put into effect. Just days after this ruling, in November 1997, Oregon's voters, forced back to the ballot box on the issue for the second time, reaffirmed their support. This time, the margin of support had grown from 51 to 60 percent of the vote, and enforcement of the measure now looked unstoppable.

The preelection campaign in this thinly populated Western state had been a nasty, no-holds-barred struggle between right-to-lifers, spearheaded by the Catholic Church, and supporters of assisted dying. This second group was headed by attorney Eli Stutsman and Measure 16's main architect, Barbara Coombs Lee, herself an attorney and a nurse, as well as executive director of the Washington-based group, Compassion in Dying.

During the campaign, the right-to-life groups picketed hospitals and individual health professionals known to support assisted death. With a campaign budget of almost $4 million, three times as much as their opponents, they also devised an aggressive media campaign of television commercials and print advertisements that, among other things, claimed that taking an overdose of drugs would only cause vomiting and further suffering, rather than the sweet oblivion promised by advocates. But voters were not to be convinced.

Observers have speculated that Oregon's initiative succeeded where California's and Washington's had failed because it was more restrictive and cautious. "A lot of people were involved in drafting the law and making sure it was what people were ready for," explains John Duncan, executive director of the Oregon Death with Dignity Legal Defense and Education Center. "It passed because it was the right law at the right time."

Whereas California's law would have let physicians administer lethal injections, the Oregon statute made provision only for allowing prescriptions for oral drugs. The measure also demanded that eligible patients must be competent to make their own decisions, and must be prepared to abide by a 2-week waiting period.

Those involved with drafting Oregon's Death with Dignity statute say they have always considered it to be a work in progress, the foundation for what they expect will be years of debate and alterations. "It's one thing to pass a law," says Arthur Caplan, director of the Center for Bioethics at the University of Pennsylvania. "It's putting it into practice that will require the real skill."

As the first step, a local panel of medical experts was set up to produce the country's first "guidebook" to assisted dying. The 91-page book, published in early 1998, recommends guidelines and safeguards to ensure the careful selection of eligible patients, and the establishment of proper procedures to help them end their lives. Among the book's stipulations: that physicians should not initiate conversations about hastening death in case they are felt to be pressuring a patient; that no physician will be forced to participate in assisting a patient to die; and that no Oregon hospice may refuse admission to a patient because of that patient's plan to pursue assisted suicide. This last provision, if initiated, will mark a real departure from traditional hospice policy, which states that while its patients may be aggressively medicated for pain, they will not be helped to die there.

One of the first areas likely to be challenged is the law's prohibition of lethal injections. Physicians wanted this provision, experts say, because they prefer the patient to be as active in his or her own death as possible, and for themselves to remain in the background. Surveys have already shown that this may not be the patient's own preference: According to a 1994 survey of Ohio residents, 54 percent of 541 people randomly questioned said they would prefer to have a physician directly involved in assisting a death. The study's author, William MacDonald, assistant professor of oncology at Ohio State University, suggests that the presence of a physician probably makes people feel more protected from abuse or bungling.

This kind of debate is almost certainly what the Supreme Court had in mind when, in June 1997, they declared the issue of assisted dying to be within the states' bailiwick rather than their own. The Court, asked to decide on the constitutional basis of two earlier state decisions, eventually concluded that hastening a person's death was not a constitutional right. It was wrong, they said, to conclude that "any and all important, intimate, and personal decisions" be automatically constitutionally protected. However, the justices made it clear that their decison should by no means be taken as the last word on the subject. "Throughout the Nation, Americans are engaged in an earnest and profound debate about the morality, legality, and practicality of physician assisted suicide," wrote Chief Justice William H. Renquist in his argument. "Our holding permits this debate to continue, as it should in a democratic society."

The Court's historic ruling on physician assisted dying came at the very end of a packed judicial session, on June 26, 1997. The justices had been considering two cases referred from the US Court of Appeals, one (*Washington v. Glucksberg*) from the Ninth Circuit, which includes Washington State, the other (*Vacco v. Quill*) from the Second Circuit, which serves New York. In these cases, the two appeals courts had agreed that terminally ill patients should be able to decide the manner and time of their death as a fundamental right guaranteed under the Fourteenth Amendment—the amendment to the U.S. Constitution guaranteeing individuals "life" and "liberty" and "equal protection" under the law. As the law stood now, they said, terminally ill but conscious patients were being denied due process, and had fewer rights than those who were being sustained through respirators or feeding tubes.

The nine Supreme Court justices were all passionately concerned about the issue at hand. All of them, in their personal lives, had lost parents and spouses to protracted diseases, or had themselves survived life-threatening illness. "This is an issue that every one of us faces, young or old, male or female, whatever it might be," said Justice Sandra Day O'Connor, who has fought her own battle against breast cancer. However, as the right-to-die attorneys began making their case, it soon became clear that most of the justices were unconvinced by the constitutional value of their arguments. Their majority decision, finding no constitutional basis for assisted dying, was widely expected. However, neither side— nor the justices themselves—wanted the debate to end there. Chief Justice Rehnquist added a footnote at the end of both case summaries to say that it was still an open question whether certain applications of the laws might impose an "intolerable intrusion on personal freedom." And he encouraged the individual states to decide the issue for themselves. Just as the justices anticipated, several states, including Michigan, Wisconsin, and Virginia, have already begun wrestling with the question. In some states, residents are trying to put the issue on their state ballots; in others, legislatures are crafting bills either to challenge existing laws, or to reinforce them. The debate is certain to continue for many years to come.

The historical landmarks of the past two decades show clearly how a popular movement takes hold within a society:

in incremental stages, step by cautious step, through the experiences of individual people played out in public arenas—the hospitals, the legislatures, and the courts. Yet activists are clear that these forums are not the place for delicate matters of life and death to be resolved. Their goal in legalizing physician aid in dying, they say, is to return the final decisions of people's lives to where they belong: the privacy of the bedside.

♦ CHAPTER 5 ♦

Foreign Rights
A World-View of Death

There is one great society alone on earth:
The noble living and the noble dead.
—William Wordsworth

In March 1997, the small European nation of the Netherlands became engrossed in an unlikely murder trial involving a popular country physician and his elderly, terminally ill patient, whom he was accused of having murdered. The physician, Sippe Schat, a general practitioner, did not contest that he had given the woman a lethal injection. But what the authorities were calling murder, Schat defined as voluntary euthanasia: The woman, who was dying of cancer, had begged him to put her out of her misery, he said. As her physician, he had complied. He had done no more than what most physicians in the Netherlands would have done—possibly most physicians throughout the world.

Indeed, while Schat was on trial, a highly respected Japanese physician, a former hospital chief, was awaiting similar proceedings in Kyoto for having given a fatal injection to a terminally ill patient. For the same crime, a Canadian physician, the first in that country to be charged with assisting a death, was facing a 14-year jail sentence in Toronto, while, across the border in Michigan, Dr. Kevorkian was preparing for his fourth assisted suicide trial.

Meanwhile, on the other side of the world in a wild and sparsely inhabited part of Australia, yet another physician had administered lethal injections to no less than three patients within a few months, using a self-programmed computer. But in his case, there was no danger of legal retribution: His home, the Northern Territory, had become the first place in the world to have legalized physicians' rights to help terminally ill patients to die. This physician, Philip Nitschke, had acted in the glare of international publicity, with the full protection of the law. But for Nitschke, it turned out to be a short respite. After just 9 months, the Australian law was repealed. Nitschke is on notice that if he helps patients to die without its protection, he, too, could find himself facing a prison term.

What is happening in the world? Have physicians (sometimes with the collusion of lawmakers) suddenly transformed themselves into murderers, as some people fear? Or is a centuries-long secret practice finally being brought out into the open? Everyone knows that physicians have always helped their suffering patients to die: The Death with Dignity Education Center estimates that it takes place in the United States about 7000 times a month. But now, suddenly, their actions are being uncovered, prosecuted, and, increasingly commonly, punished. Assisted death, in all parts of the world, is being conscientiously reassessed.

There was a time when physicians found guilty of so-called mercy killing were given a token suspended sentence and a nod of tacit respect. But within the past several years, societies seem to be taking a harsher view of the act. In 1992, British physician Nigel Cox was suspended from practicing medicine for a year while awaiting trial, and then found guilty of attempted murder for giving a 70-year-old dying patient, Lillian Boyes, a lethal injection to end weeks of agonizing pain. Cox had been Boyes's physician for 13 years, and had acted to the relief and appreciation of both the patient and her family. Despite widespread public support of his action, Cox was given a 12-month suspended sentence—a verdict that shocked many with its harshness.

In the Netherlands, Sippe Schat was also treated harshly. He was imprisoned for 2 weeks before his trial, and then, to the shock of the Dutch public, made to face the most severe possible penalty for his crime—12 years or more in jail. Ironically, given the legal climate in Holland, Schat need never have been prosecuted at all. Although assisted death and euthanasia are officially illegal in that country, both practices have been openly accepted for over 20 years, so long as certain guidelines, established in 1984 by the Dutch Medical Association, are applied. If physicians adhere to the guidelines when they perform euthanasia, they are immune from prosecution.

But Schat had chosen to ignore them: Although his patient, a 72-year-old woman, had been fully competent to make her own decision—one of the foremost official requirements—he had not asked her to put her request for death in writing before he helped her, nor had he submitted a formal notification to the local medical officer, or consulted with two independent colleagues—all of which he was obliged to do under the regulations. What's more, Schat falsified the patient's death certificate by writing that her death had resulted from natural causes. Perhaps most shocking of all, after having injected a lethal dose of morphine and insulin into her veins, he had apparently left his patient alone to die. Schat's lawyer, Willem Anker, admits that although his client unwisely ignored the rules, his motivation—to help a suffering, incurable patient—was nonetheless not in question. "The most important thing is that he is not accused of murder," Anker said before the trial.

One reason why there was a call for such severe punishment, commentators suggested, is because the government needed to make it clear that the rules for carrying out euthanasia must be taken seriously. Dr. Bob Smalhout, lecturer, newspaper commentator, and professor of anesthesiology, resuscitation, and intensive care at the University of Utrecht, believes that, at a time when Holland's euthanasia policy is being increasingly criticized for its abuses and lack of accountability, Schat was being used as an example, to make a public statement.

"Everyone thinks that this case is a warning," Smalhout told me at the time. "A warning for physicians to tread very carefully, or the government or one's colleagues can use your actions as a weapon against you."

In recent years, there has been a growing body of criticism about the misuse of euthanasia in the Netherlands. As the right-to-die movement around the world has grown, Holland has come under increasingly close international scrutiny. In response, the government has put measures in place to try to regulate the practice more tightly. As the only country openly practicing physician-assisted dying, the Netherlands is increasingly viewed as a blueprint for the rest of the world. And nowadays, virtually every country in the world, confronted with aging populations, shrinking medical budgets, and life-prolonging technology, seems to be looking for a model that works. What all of them want to know is: Can an advanced society steeped in the medical doctrine of death as defeat end prolonged suffering without compromising its ethical underpinnings? And can suffering people be given the help they crave without bestowing on physicians a power that is intimidating, both in its magnitude and in its potential for abuse?

In some countries, the simple answer is no. There can be no individual right to die in cultures dominated by powerfully opposed religions: Roman Catholicism, orthodox Judaism, Mormonism, Islam. In countries ruled by these faiths, there is no room for debate, as the notion of controlling death undermines religion's most fundamental tenet: that life is sacred at all stages, that (for some faiths) suffering is ennobling, and that no one but God has the right to bring life to a close.

But most countries operate under more secularized and pragmatic systems of governance. In several, such as Britain, Canada, Greece, Finland, Norway, and the United States—countries with similar democratic, ecumenical structures—the desire to adopt right-to-die laws has strong popular support. In Canada especially, opinion polls show a national approval rate for aid in dying of 72 percent—higher than either the United States or Britain—and in the provinces of Quebec and British Columbia, it can reach as high as 80 percent. "That's probably as high as the figures can go, given that there will always be some opposition," says John Hofsess, director of the Canadian Right to Die Society.

In Britain, where there has been an active euthanasia society for more than 50 years and no fewer than six parliamentary attempts this century to decriminalize assisted death, popular support is also on the rise. In summer 1997, two British physicians admitted to the press their role in dozens of assisted deaths in the course of their careers, and no action was finally taken against them. Later that same year, Annie Lindsell, a 47-year-old right-to-die campaigner in the last stages of Lou Gehrig's disease (known as motor neuron disease in Britain) brought a highly publicized action to the British High Court to win her doctor the right to give her a lethal injection of diamorphine, should she end up suffocating to death, as she feared. Although Lindsell finally died without aid in December 1997, the court did recognize her right to painkillers to alleviate her suffering, even if they brought about her death, and her doctor had publicly declared himself willing to take whatever action she needed—no matter what the outcome. It was a groundbreaking case, and Lindsell's fellow campaigners, a group of eight seriously ill people, swore to continue her fight one by one, as each of them faced their own deaths. Meanwhile, the membership of the British Voluntary Euthanasia Society swelled.

Even China has shown strong approval for the idea: According to a survey by China's official news agency, support for assisted dying in the three largest cities is as high as 78 percent, and in Shanghai, an astounding 90 percent. Perhaps that is not surprising in a country with the world's largest aging population; 100 million Chinese are already aged 60 or older, and every day 20,000 more reach that age. (China even has its own version of Dr. Kevorkian—a 74-year-old activist and physician, Wu Zhaoguang, who has been petitioning the central Beijing government for the past 10 years to be allowed to set up carefully regulated euthanasia clinics around the country. So far, he has not been granted permission.)

Despite the popular appeal of the idea, however, most governments have been reluctant to make it law—even China, renowned for its strict policies in population control.

The example of Australia is probably the most useful one for the United States to study, because as a large continent with individual, self-governing territories, the practical mechanics of state lawmaking are familar to us.

In 1995, Australia's most remote region, the Northern Territory, approved an assisted suicide law. Opponents immediately challenged it and managed to tie it up in court for over a year. It came into effect in 1996, and for a brief period of 8 months, until it was repealed, Australia became the only place on earth where assisted death was legal.

The most unusual aspect of this particular law is that its impetus came from a politician, not from the people. Unlike other political leaders who have shown reluctance in opening such a potential tinderbox, Marshall Perron, for 15 years the uncontested Conservative Chief Minister of the Northern Territory, introduced his assisted suicide statute in 1994 as his final legislative act before retirement. He presented it in a form that allowed his parliamentary colleagues to vote freely according to their own consciences. But Perron's closest ally, physician Philip Nitschke, believes it only passed (by the slimmest of margins, 13 to 12) as a tribute to the retiring leader.

"When he decided to link his retirement to this legislation, people felt they should do something for him, to show their appreciation," Nitschke says. "I think they voted for his bill as a kind of going away present for him." Perron chose to see the victory as representing something loftier. "I said after the successful vote, 'It's good to know democracy is alive and the conscience vote still means something,'" Perron told an enthusiastic audience at the World Federation of Right to Die Societies in Melbourne in October 1996.

The Northern Territory is a rugged state about twice the size of Texas, with vast expanses of open land and a sparse population of 18,000 made up of tough, modern-day settlers, determined to run their society according to their own rules. This is one reason, according to Nitschke, why the politicians voted such a controversial statute into force. "They wanted to show the rest of the country that they go their own way," Nitschke says.

The rest of the country responded to the law with bitter divisiveness. For some, its adoption was seen as the action of a truly progressive government, farsighted enough to update its laws in response to the new demands of an advanced society.

Two people from this group benefited directly from the law. As the first two people to be legally helped to die by a physician, 66-year-old Bob Dent and 52-year-old Janet Mills both left letters behind at their deaths, reaffirming their support.

"If you disagree with voluntary euthanasia, then don't use it, but please don't deny the right to me," wrote Dent.

"I hope this law survives and is able to help others like me, who has found the suffering has become too great," added Mills, who was helped to die a few weeks after Dent. "It should not be overturned by the politicians in Canberra, but given a chance to be made to work in the way it was intended. I want people to see just how important this law was to me now that I'm at the end of my life."

But, with some 400 more terminal patients reported to be standing by to use the act, opponents predicted that the state would become the "killing capital of the world."

Among the fiercest of the Act's opponents were members of the Northern Territory medical community. Surveys at the time showed that they were far more opposed than the population at large; in an open letter to the local press, 14 medical specialists declared that they would "in no way" involve themselves with the Act. In a region with just a couple hundred physicians, their widespread refusal to cooperate— by adding a required second signature to a patient's request form—threatened to make the legislation unworkable. "Physicians have just about wrecked it," Nitschke said at the time, as both Dent and Mills were forced to wait for supportive physicians to come forward. "Even those who support the principle don't want to become too closely associated with it, because it's all such a damn mess." A spokesman for the Coalition of Voluntary Euthanasia Organizations added that the physicians' declaration of opposition was an example of the "outrageous" pressure placed on them by the Australian Medical Association not to cooperate with the new law.

The furor spread far beyond the territory's boundaries to engulf the country. Sydney's Catholic archbishop, Edward Clancy, termed Dent's death "a shameful day for Australia," while at the federal government level, Liberal Senator Kevin

Andrews, an ardent Christian, immediately put forward a bill in the federal Senate, a higher legislature with powers to overturn laws made in the lower house, to quash the aid-in-dying law. Andrews campaigned hard and on March 29, 1997, federal senators voted 38 to 34 to overturn the Northern Territory's 1995 Rights of the Terminally Ill Act. The Act immediately became invalid, leaving at least two terminally ill patients thwarted in their efforts to seek a physician-assisted death. Despite their completed paperwork (including signatures from the requisite two additional physicians), the state's governor general, Sir William Deane, refused the patients' plea for a special exemption to allow them time to carry out their chosen fate.

Ironically, a national opinion poll published around the same time showed that Australians' support of the right-to-die was at an all-time high of 70 percent. And a major new survey of 3000 physicians (carried out by Monash University and published internationally on the Internet by the *Medical Journal of Australia*) showed that 30 percent of deaths in Australia are the result of deliberate end-of-life decisions by physicians. Just over 5 percent of them—an estimated 37,000—are caused by "euthanasia without consent," causing the study's chief author, Helga Kuhse, professor of human bioethics at Monash University, to conclude that "Australian law has not prevented physicians from practising euthanasia or making medical end-of-life decisions explicitly intended to hasten death without the patient's request."

Since the demise of the Northern Territory statute, leg-islators from other parts of Australia have been attempting to introduce similar laws. None has so far had success, but Nitschke has announced that he will move wherever assisted dying becomes legal, in order to continue his work. He has little hope of progress for a long time to come, yet whatever happens in the future, he says, he will always look on the passage of the territory's Act with a great sense of achieve-ment.

"This event will one day become seen as an incident in time when it was shown, briefly, that such a law is possible and workable, and a number of people can get from it the help that they seek. What's more," he adds, "the sky doesn't fall because of it."

For the Dutch, the evolution and acceptance of euthanasia have been far less traumatic—perhaps in keeping with the national character. The Netherlands is a tolerant and easy-going country, where unconventional lifestyles coexist com-fortably with a bourgeois, middle-class way of life. Over the past several decades, the Dutch people have painlessly ab-sorbed a hippie culture into their main cities, in which many people openly use drugs on the streets. Prostitutes sit and sell their wares in the windows of "red-light districts" in the center of town, and euthanasia has become an accepted ser-vice for the country's medical profession. Although officially illegal, all three practices—drug use, prostitution, and, in particular, euthanasia—are tolerated within Dutch society, and protected by a body of case law and strong popular support. Most citizens, and a majority of physicians, claim to be at ease with the principle.

But Dutch society has two significant elements that contribute to that ease. First, all patients are attended by "huisarts"—family physicians like Schat who have close, long-term relationships with patients and their families. Up to the time of being charged with murder in early 1996, Schat had led a kind of storybook existence as a general practitioner in a small rural community in northern Holland. He had a comfortable house that came with his job, and a practice of 2000 devoted patients. According to those patients, he was a committed and kindly family physician who worked long hours, opened his home-cum-office to those who needed him at any time of the day, and visited those unable to come to him—the sickest of them sometimes two or three times a day. The woman he had euthanized had been a patient for years. (In fact, Schat was so popular that when he was removed from his practice, his patients refused to go to any other physician. They were thwarted, however, when the local insurance company declined to reimburse them for his treatments.)

"Mostly, our physicians, when they perform euthanasia on their patients, have known them on average seven or more years and the specialists have known them for about two years or more," says Herbert Barnard, the health attaché at the Netherlands Embassy in Washington, D.C. This kind of health care is in marked contrast to the kind of care Americans tend to receive, especially when they are very sick and probably in hospital. There, the numerous white-coated strangers who pass by their bedside know virtually nothing about them save their physical symptoms.

The second factor in Holland's relationship with assisted dying is that the country's comprehensive national health care coverage provides every citizen with medical care, from infant immunizations to nursing homes. No one has to fear being deprived of health care because of cost—a major worry for Americans, especially the 43 million who are currently uninsured. In Holland, the concern that assisted dying could be encouraged for economic reasons simply does not apply.

This is not to say, however, that euthanasia has been without problems in that country. Long before Schat was accused of murder, the authorities knew that physicians were not complying strictly enough with their regulations. What's more, no one was keeping reliable statistics. So in 1990, the government appointed a special commission headed by the attorney general of the Dutch Supreme Court, Professor Jan Remmelink, to carry out a confidential survey of physicians' end-of-life practices. Remmelink's researchers found that over 50 percent of the nation's physicians practiced euthanasia, and of 130,000 annual deaths in the country, 49,000 involved some kind of medical procedure, such as withholding or removing life support or alleviating pain with medications also known to hasten death—the "double effect." Of the total number, 2300 deaths (1.8 percent) were caused by euthanasia and 400 (0.3 percent) were the result of assisted suicide. In nearly all of these 2700 deaths, the guidelines had been met, which meant that the physicians who carried out the procedures would not be prosecuted.

However, the commission learned that, like Schat, the vast majority of physicians who performed euthanasia did not report it, tending to list the cause of death as being related to natural causes. A 1995 follow-up study showed that in recent years, the reporting procedures had "substantially" improved. Nevertheless, a full 59 percent of euthanasia deaths were still not being accurately reported.

The study also found that in addition to the 2700 legitimate euthanasia deaths that had taken place, there were a further 1000 cases (0.8 percent) where the patient had not been competent when euthanasia had been performed—a clear violation of the government guidelines.

Critics of the Dutch system are appalled by these figures, concluding that physicians are making independent decisions about whether a patient will live or die, and then carrying them out without consulting the patient. But health attaché Barnard claims that quoting the figures without explaining their circumstances misrepresents them. "In 91 percent of these cases, the patient's life was shortened by only a few hours or maybe a couple of days—we are talking about patients in the final stages of life, clearly suffering," Barnard says. "And in 53 percent of these cases, euthanasia *was* discussed with the patient, even though the discussions weren't concluded." Of the remaining 47 percent, he says, the majority (79 percent) were no longer competent to make the request because they were suffering from either intense pain or dementia. "The physician wasn't making the decision alone," Barnard explains. "He had mostly discussed it with the patient's family and/or a colleague. It is not something a physician takes lightly."

There is one more area of concern. Critics charge that despite clear parameters set out by the Royal Dutch Medical Association, euthanasia has sometimes been performed on patients who were ineligible under the country's qualifying criteria: comatose patients, severely deformed babies, and, in some cases, people who were not physically ill, but who chose not to live any longer. Despite prosecutions, the physicians involved were not punished. One involved a man in his 40s who was HIV positive but had not yet developed any symptoms of AIDS. Another case involved a gynecologist who, at the parents' request, euthanized their 3-day old daughter who was born with a partially undeveloped brain, spina bifida, and partial paralysis, and was diagnosed as having just weeks to live.

"Euthanasia as we understand it has to be asked for by a patient," said the legal advisor of the Royal Dutch Medical Association, speaking for the prosecution. Nevertheless, the public prosecutor finally decided not to bring charges.

The most controversial of all recent cases concerned a healthy 50-year-old woman given the pseudonym "Netty Boomsma." Boomsma was referred to a prominent psychiatrist, Dr. Boudewijn Chabot, in July 1991, two months after her 20-year-old son had died of cancer. A few years earlier, her elder son had committed suicide, also at the age of 20.

Now, divorced from the boys' father and deeply grieving for her children, the woman wanted to commit suicide so she could join them, as she put it. She had had the two boys buried together, and had bought the space between them for her own grave.

"I am not religious, but everything is so senseless, so empty, so useless," the woman wrote in a letter to Chabot. "The grief, the despair, it is all so terrible."

Boomsma had already seen other psychologists. She had tried, unsuccessfully, to commit suicide once, and she now refused to take antidepressants or undergo more counseling. Chabot promised her that if she entered wholeheartedly into therapy with him, he would agree to help her die if, at the end of their sessions, she still did not feel any will to go on living. She agreed. The two spent a total of 30 hours in session over that summer, and Chabot also talked with Boomsma's sister and brother-in-law, who were close to her and loved her. At the end of August, Boomsma said she didn't want any more meetings: She had not changed her mind, and she wanted to die. She asked Chabot if he would help her. If not, she said, she would kill herself.

Chabot consulted a number of colleagues. Although one recommended bereavement therapy, all of the others agreed with Chabot that therapy had very little prospect of helping her. After meeting with her a couple more times, he finally agreed to give her a prescription for lethal drugs. On September 27, Chabot and a colleague were present to witness Boomsma sprinkle the contents of the capsules into a bowl of custard, eat them, and then lay down in the bedroom of her younger son, on his bed, clutching a photograph of her two children. Within half an hour, she was dead.

Chabot went to trial for his role in helping Netty Boomsma to die, a trial that took all day before a panel of three judges. (There are no jury trials in the Netherlands.) The prosecutor asked for a 1-year conditional sentence, meaning that if found guilty, Chabot would serve a year in prison if he were to repeat his crime. In the end, the judges acquitted Chabot on the grounds that a patient's psychological suffering was as valid a reason for seeking euthanasia as physical suffering. The case was referred first to an appeals court and later to the Dutch Supreme Court. Both agreed with the finding.

For critics, the Boomsma case, more than any other, exemplifies the argument of the "slippery slope."

"The Netherlands has moved from assisted suicide to euthanasia, from euthanasia for people who are terminally ill to euthanasia for those who are chronically ill, from euthanasia for physical illness to euthanasia for psychological distress, and from voluntary euthanasia to involuntary euthanasia (called 'termination of the patient without explicit request')," says Herbert Hendin in his book *Seduced by Death: Physicians, Patients, and the Dutch Cure.* "Virtually every guideline established by the Dutch to regulate euthanasia has been modified or violated with impunity. . . . What the Dutch intended was supposedly an extreme measure in extreme cases, but it has become the easy alternative—almost a routine way of dealing with serious illness, and even depression," he says.

For Hendin, Boomsma's request—along with too many others—was carried out without sufficient attempts to help the patient confront her fear and grief. He suggests a number of options that he would have tried for the grieving woman, from simply allowing time to blunt her grief, to engaging her in social work or a project devoted to youth suicide prevention. "Her last words to Chabot—'Why do young kids want suicide?'—suggests that work which permitted her to deal with that question might have meaningfully engaged her in a way that would have been more positive for her as well as for those she might have helped," he writes.

These complex cases from the Netherlands have given rise to much analysis. Interestingly, the figures and the individual stories tend to be taken—like Rorschach inkblots—to support whatever viewpoint the interpreter favors. Proponents claim that assisted death has helped end the suffering of many desperate dying people, that it is requested three times more often than it is used, and that the numbers being euthanized have remained constant over the years. Opponents say that the practice has gotten out of hand, as strict profiles of eligibility have been ignored and patients have sometimes been "euthanized" without consent. All of these violations, critics say, are clear illustrations of the real dangers of the slippery slope.

What the Dutch experience also highlights is the universal fallibility of human beings: that some people—even physicians—can be ill-advised, hasty, careless, mistaken, and even too arrogant. "Schat's mistake was that he was a real old-fashioned physician—he thought he was next to God," says Smalhout. Physicians can also be mistaken and careless when they're diagnosing, performing surgery, aiding childbirth. Unfortunately, people die needlessly in all kinds of medical circumstances. Yet none of it happens by design.

In the end, the sentence Schat received may reflect the Dutch awareness of this fact. Although he was prepared to go to jail, the judges imposed a 6-month suspended sentence and a reprimand for "unprofessional conduct." Nonetheless, Schat had lost an enormous amount during his ordeal. His practice had been dismantled, his patient load spread among other physicians, and he was no longer entitled to his home, which was tied to the job. He moved away from northern Holland and has settled in Amsterdam. He currently makes a living by acting as a locum for colleagues who go on holiday or fall ill.

The problems in Holland, the legal battles in Australia, the defiant confessions of physicians in many other countries, and the halfhearted, unregulated attempts to control the practice, all point to the same thing: that whether it is legal or illegal, condoned or condemned, people worldwide remain deeply conflicted about the morality of assisted death. They are unsure whether they stand at the top of a slippery slope, looking down, or at its base, looking up to higher, more humane ground. No country has yet found a faultless way to end suffering. But all over the world, people are struggling to find solutions.

CHAPTER 6

Dr. Death
Dispensing Mercy or Murder?

Verse, Fame and Beauty are intense indeed,
But Death intenser—Death is Life's high Meed.
                                    —Keats

February 18, 1993—the day when 41-year-old Martha
Ruwart was going to die—dawned cold and snowy in subur-
ban Michigan. Martha, or Martie as she was known, lay sick
and frail on a living room sofa. Her insides were riddled with
duodenal and ovarian cancer, and she had suffered an agonizing decline over two long, difficult years. Now, she was
anxious to have it all over with at last. "Let's do it," she said.
But the man who was presiding over her death, Dr. Jack
Kevorkian, wasn't to be hurried. Calm and controlled, he
talked for a little while, handed her the consent form to sign,
and reassured her that if at any time she wanted to back out,
she could. She could always try again at a later time. Martie
said no, she was quite ready. So the five people who had ac-

companied her—her three sisters, Teresa Post, Karen Swindell, and Mary Ruwart, and her lifelong friends, Gary and Bernadette Fairfax—each had a private moment to kiss Martie and say good-bye. Then she put on and adjusted a plastic mask, which had airholes so that she could breathe oxygen. A tube with a clip connected the mask to a carbon monoxide cylinder. This contraption was Dr. Kevorkian's celebrated Mercitron—the machine that he had designed to help dying patients deliver a lethal dose of carbon monoxide to themselves. Kevorkian tied one end of a string to the clip, and the other end to Martie's finger. He told her that when she was ready, she could pull the string to release the carbon monoxide. She was ready—she pulled. Then, with each breath she took, carbon monoxide seeped into her body. She choked a little, as Kevorkian had warned she would. A few minutes later, she was dead.

Martie Ruwart was the 14th person Jack Kevorkian had helped to die. Earlier that same morning, another fatally ill person, 44-year-old Jonathon Grenz, had died in a back bedroom in the same house. Grenz had been suffering from mouth, neck, and chest cancer. Their deaths marked the fourth double suicide that Kevorkian had arranged. Immediately afterwards, in response, the Michigan governor, John Engler, signed a new bill into law that made assisted suicide illegal—starting at once.

All over the country, the members of the many right-to-die groups are unanimous in acknowledging that, if it weren't for Jack Kevorkian—Dr. Death, as the media is so fond of calling him—their cause would not now be in the headlines and before the highest court in the land. Kevorkian has single-handedly done more to highlight the issue of physician-assisted suicide than anyone else in the world.

In his Salvation Army cardigans, with his skull-like face and flamboyant temper, this bizarre character has become one of the country's most recognizable celebrities, as well known to the general public as any politician or movie star. And he may be more popular than many of those: in a recent opinion poll, 68 percent of people said they approved of his actions.

Without doubt, Kevorkian is a complex symbol of the issues under debate: a man who, as his actions have shown, is willing "to put my money where my mouth is," and who's prepared, so he claims, to die for the principles for which he is fighting.

Kevorkian is revered as a near saint by his supporters, abhorred as a mass murderer by his opponents. A loner and a nonconformist, people who know him say he's also gentle, humorous, and compassionate; juries have three times refused to convict him of murder or misconduct, and scores of people continue to cross the country for his help in dying.

Meanwhile in his home state of Michigan, Kevorkian has been stalked by a gunman, denounced by the Catholic Church and disabled groups, and pursued by law enforcers sworn to curtailing his activities. Over the years, the Oakland County chief medical examiner, Dr. Ljubisa Dragovic, and the former county prosecutor, Richard Thompson, have been waging what has become virtually a private feud to try to stop Kevorkian in his tracks. Dragovic insists that there is nothing personal about his vendetta, that his goal is simply to carry out his job, not to persecute Kevorkian. "I don't want to see him go to prison—I want to see him in a psychiatric institution," he says. "He's out to lunch—he's been out to lunch for most of his life. Between that wacko, and the group of people surrounding him who are in it for the money, this whole thing is a charade, a circus, masked by the proclamation of people fighting for the right to die."

The struggle with public prosecutor Richard Thompson, however, took on more obsessive dimensions for both men. In August 1996, when Thompson lost a Republican election primary, his defeat was widely regarded as a public referendum on his continuing witch hunt of Kevorkian. (His rival, Dave Gorcyca, promised that if elected, he would not spend public funds prosecuting Kevorkian.) But Thompson had one last weapon to use against his nemesis before he disappeared: In October 1996, just a matter of weeks before leaving office, the outgoing prosecutor brought another, final, round of criminal charges down on Kevorkian's head. This time, Thompson indicted the physician on 19 counts, including helping three women to die during the summer of 1996, possessing a controlled substance (the medication with which they were injected), improperly posing as a physician (because his medical license has been forfeited by the state), and improperly moving bodies (by taking them from their place of death to either the hospital or the medical examiner's office).

Kevorkian, appearing at Michigan's 48th District Court to answer the charges, called the prosecutor "a lying psychotic" and said that, this time, "Either Thompson dies or I die, by which I mean, either this dies as a legal issue or I do, and I don't care which, but this ends now." If imprisoned, Kevorkian swore to start a hunger strike, and maintain it until death. He had embarked on a hunger strike once before, when imprisoned and awaiting trial back in 1992. After 18 days, he was released from jail and taken, in a weakened state, to the local hospital.

As it turned out, such histrionics were not necessary this time. As one of his first acts in office, Dave Gorcyca remained true to his campaign promise and dropped all 19 of the charges against Kevorkian. Gorcyca said that prosecuting him in his home county was "an exercise in futility," and that he wasn't prepared to waste taxpayers' money when he had already seen that no jury was prepared to indict him.

To qualify to be a "patient" of Dr. Kevorkian, you have to travel to Michigan to see him, as the physician claims he is too afraid to fly. As a result, he has squarely placed on the map a small corner of middle America that was not designed with fame—or notoriety—in mind. Oakland County, where Kevorkian lives in a small, spartan apartment, is a quiet, fairly affluent township just north of Detroit, best known until 1990 for its swanky Somerset shopping mall and the Pontiac Silverdome, home of the Detroit Lions. Today, the county courthouse, its hospitals, and even its motels are landmarks in the strange odyssey of an unlikely American original.

It was in 1990 that Jack Kevorkian first went on the *Phil Donahue Show* to let the world know that he was in the "Obitiatry" business, prepared to perform "medicide" or "patholysis" on any terminally suffering person who might want it. Since then, at least 100 people have taken him up on his offer.

But the physician has done more than that: Not content simply to help terminally ill people to end their life weeks or even months before its natural end, Kevorkian has challenged society to accept an even more radical idea. He has also helped those with long-term chronic conditions like Alzheimer's disease and multiple sclerosis to die, people who are not technically in the process of dying, but who want to be freed from the slow inevitability of physical decline. According to Dragovic, of the 36 Kevorkian patients whose bodies he has been called on to autopsy (at the time of writing), just 10 exhibited symptoms of "terminal illness" (officially, defined as an illness presenting the prognosis of 6 months or less to live). Another 23 were found to have "anatomically present diseases," although they were not near the point of death, and 3 others showed no sign of disease at all.

One of these was Rebecca Badger, a 39-year-old California woman who traveled to Michigan to seek Kevorkian's help in ending 8 years of physical suffering diagnosed by her California physician as multiple sclerosis. But Dragovic says that autopsy findings revealed a robust, physically fit young woman. "I looked at her brain tissue, her brain stem, her spinal cord and her optic nerves and found nothing, nothing at all," Dragovic says. "She was a still young woman with a neurotic conversion—a psychiatric condition where unresolved conflicts or frustrations get converted into physical symptoms that focus on a particular part of the body. That type of condition can frequently simulate multiple sclerosis, which is often very hard to diagnose." In the wake of the autopsy, Badger's physician, contacted by *People*, said, "Looking backward and looking at the autopsy, this woman died of a psychiatric disease."

Another recent patient, 42-year-old Judith Curren, was also determined to be not fatally ill. Curren, who weighed 265 pounds, suffered from a muscle disorder called fibromyalgia and from chronic fatigue syndrome. But although she was bedridden and had complained of insufferable pain for over a decade, critics, including her own physicians, ventured that her most acute problem was depression. Background checks also revealed that she had been beaten on a couple of occasions by her husband, a charge he later denied.

The implication that Kevorkian knew Curren wasn't physically ill, or that he had helped Curren's husband to "dispose of" her, was blasted by Kevorkian's lawyer, Geoffrey Fieger, at one of the many press conferences he holds at his offices each time his client takes some new action. "Does Dr. Dragovic have no shame?" Fieger thundered. "This was *her* decision. What does it take with you people? Why do you repeat these lies? It is an outrage!" he said. (Fieger jokes that if ever he is diagnosed with a terminal disease, he will go to Dragovic for a second opinion.)

Nevertheless, it is this straining at the leash, this pushing up against the outer limits of social acceptability, that has so shocked the authorities and Kevorkian's opponents. Lately, his rapidly rising death toll—at a press conference in early 1998, Kevorkian announced that it had reached 100— has even angered some supporters, the more conservative reformers who are anxious to convince public opinion that the legalizing of physician-assisted death would *not* amount to carte blanche for anyone who decided he wanted to die.

Yet the families of his "patients" remain loyal and grateful. Although Christy Nichols, Rebecca Badger's daughter, now wonders whether her mother could have been cured, she still regards Kevorkian as "an angel." Virginia Bernero, whose dying son consulted Kevorkian, testified at his first trial that the physician was "a wonderful, caring man. I don't think he has a mean bone in his body." And Carol Poenisch, the daughter of Merion Fredricks, whom Kevorkian helped to die in 1993, says she will always be grateful to the man who enabled her mother to have "a model death."

Mary Ruwart and her family still see Kevorkian's role in their lives as that of a saint who saved their beloved sister, Martie, from a horrible and agonizing death.

"Martie was more afraid of being in pain, with her mind no longer intact, than she was of death," said her sister, Mary.

For Martie, the existence of Dr. Kevorkian became important several weeks before she actually chose to die. At the beginning of January 1993, when she knew her final downward path had begun, she asked her family to contact him. Her sister Teresa and her husband, Pete, pored over old newspaper articles, figuring out how to get in touch. They saw that Kevorkian lived in Royal Oak, then simply called directory assistance to get his telephone number. (The number is no longer listed.) Teresa asked him if Martie could be his patient. He told her to forward Martie's medical information and a physician's report on her mental competence. The sisters did it by overnight mail.

On the night of Tuesday, February 9, Martie was in severe distress. She had vomited four or five times and her strength was spent. She cried, "It's time to call Dr. Kevorkian and make an appointment." Although it was late in the evening, the doctor took the call. Mary put him on the speaker phone and he talked to Martie in a considerate, yet strong and forceful voice. Martie was desperate. She said she wanted to go the very next day, but Kevorkian explained that it would take longer than that, and he encouraged her to use the time to think hard about her choice. But Martie replied, "I won't take no for an answer. I've made up my mind and I need you. Please don't say no or back out on me." Kevorkian agreed he'd be there for her. He said he would help her to die the following Saturday.

As soon as Kevorkian had agreed to help, Mary recalls, Martie's spirits lifted remarkably. She had been bedridden for a month and hadn't wanted any visitors. All of a sudden, she was able to sit up for part of the day and she became more sociable. She could barely eat a thing, but she'd stopped vomiting. Her extreme tension abated. She began to relax and said she felt so changed, she wondered if she'd need Dr. Kevorkian at all. Mary mentioned this change to him. He said that it seemed to happen to almost all of his patients. He said that for many people, the fear of suffering was so great that it overwhelmed them, and that once they knew there was another option, they instantly felt better. "It's like insurance," Kevorkian said. "The insurance I offer is that you don't have to die in pain. That relieves them, and many then go on to die from the disease."

The one thing that Dr. Kevorkian still needed from the Ruwart family was a house where she could die. And because he won't travel far, the house needed to be in the area. It couldn't be Mary's home, as Kevorkian refused to assist suicides in rental accommodation. It couldn't be the home of Teresa or Karen, because their husbands were worried about legal repercussions. So when Martie's father said they could come to his house, everything seemed to be set.

But a couple of days before the scheduled date, their father changed his mind; he said he was afraid he'd have bad memories. His children were furious with him, and Martie once again became very anxious and disappointed. "But at least her disappointment helped her to be sure," Mary said. "Martie said that it made her realize that suicide was really what she wanted, and that she was entirely ready for it."

As the search for a suitable house continued, Martie mulled over her other options for ending her life. An overdose of medicine would be very hard for her as she had so much difficulty keeping anything down. She considered shooting herself, but the idea of blowing her body to pieces terrified her. She debated sitting in a running car in a closed garage, but that would require someone to put her in the car and turn on the ignition, and that could lead to charges of homicide. The options were all traumatic, for everyone. Then, at the last minute, Dr. Kevorkian came up with a suitable venue—the home of his assistant, Neil Nicol, a couple of hours' drive away.

The evening before the scheduled day for Martie's death, Martie, her three sisters, and two good friends drove to a motel in Waterford, Michigan. There, Mary Ruwart washed her sister's hair and put makeup on her drawn face. "She looked pretty good, considering her condition," Mary said. Then Dr. Kevorkian, accompanied by his sister, Margo Janus, and his assistant, Neil, arrived at the motel. He had come to meet Martie, to ensure that this was what she really wanted, and to videotape her consent—as he does with all of the people he helps. He was upbeat and quite playful with Martie, her sister recalled. "When we were making the tape, Dr. Kevorkian said, 'Well now, we've talked about my fee, haven't we? and Martie and I looked at each other, confused. Then he laughed and said, 'Yes, my fee—it's nothing, yes!'"

Mary Ruwart said that throughout their meeting, Kevorkian treated Martie with the utmost compassion and caring. "It was clear to me that this man is dedicated to helping others," she said. "I don't think he has any hidden agenda. I'm certain that if he had seen a different solution for Martie, he would have suggested it." (Kevorkian has suggested alternative solutions for some of his patients. For example, he sent Janet Adkins, his first patient, away for a few months to try more medical options before he finally agreed to help her.)

The Ruwarts and their friends had decided to be as loving and upbeat as they could that final evening—there was no sense being morose, they felt, and after all of the complications, things had finally fallen into place: Martie was getting her wish. The group had thought they would stay awake for much of the night, talking and watching the 20 years' worth of old home movies that their friend Gary had brought along with him. But Martie was so exhausted after the meeting with Kevorkian that she went straight to bed. The others followed soon after.

The next morning, Dr. Kevorkian's sister, Margo, arrived at the motel to pick them all up. She was crying, and at first, the Ruwarts thought that something had gone wrong with their plan. But she assured them all was well. She said she was crying for the man whom her brother had just helped to die. It was always so wrenching, she said, as she helped Martie into her car.

Finally, on the sofa of Neil Nicol's home, Martie's journey came to end. With Dr. Kevorkian and her loved ones by her side, she breathed in carbon monoxide from a mask and began sliding toward unconsciousness. For a moment or two, she was still able to talk to her sisters. She said it was stuffy inside the mask and she felt as if she were drifting off to sleep. Then she became silent. Gary asked whether she could still hear them, and she said, "Yes, but you're really far away. I think this is the last time I'll be talking to you." Everyone stood by silently as she stopped breathing. At the very end, she had a few convulsions, as Dr. Kevorkian had explained that she would. Then she was still.

For the family, the hardest part of Martie's death was its aftermath, as the emergency services swooped down on Nicol's house and removed Martie's body for an autopsy. Kevorkian's lawyer, Fieger, arrived and dealt with police questions, so the Ruwarts didn't have to do that. Nevertheless, Mary said, "I felt violated by the authorities. They interfered with our mourning in a way that was unnecessary and cruel."

A few hours later, however, Mary agreed to talk to the press about what had happened that day. She chose to do so, she said, because she wanted to help Dr. Kevorkian's work, and because she wanted her sister Martie's death to count for something: She thought Martie would be proud if her death could help the cause of physician-assisted suicide. "I'm proud that Martie accomplished something important with her death," Mary concluded. "She showed others who are terminally ill that dying with dignity is possible."

But in the 5 years since Ruwart's death, critics say, Kevorkian's patients have not found such dignified ends. They criticize the physician's tactics of leaving bodies in parking lots, outside hospitals or mortuaries, or in hotel rooms. And they are outraged that the press and public have become so inured to Kevorkian's practices that a Kevorkian death barely merits a paragraph in a national newspaper anymore. "The selling of Kevorkian and the distortion of his program constitute a failure of a lazy, sloppy and biased press," wrote Michael Betzold in "The Selling of Doctor Death," an article that appeared in the *New Republic* in May 1997.

It is certainly fascinating that, for all of the national attention focused on Jack Kevorkian over the last several years, his strange personality—part curmudgeon, part messiah—remains a mystery to all but his innermost circle. People say he's on a mission, yet he insists he's not. He is so convinced of the rightness of his work that he seems almost supercilious when asked to account for his behavior in court or to the press. It is clear that he shows two very different sides of his nature to those he assists and those he opposes. Those he opposes happen to include the conventional medical profession ("insane"), law enforcement officers ("Nazi storm troopers"), legislators ("lying"), religious leaders ("irrational"), and, most particularly, the media ("meretricious wimps"). He lambasted all of the above when he made a rare public appearance at a National Press Club luncheon in Washington in July, 1996. It is this kind of blunt talk, and his refusal to compromise for the sake of a squeamish public, that add to the somewhat distasteful impression Kevorkian leaves. "I've heard him described as being like a little boy who never outgrew the desire to pull the wings off flies," pathologist Dragovic says. "I have to agree with that, looking at the man's professional life. How to terminate people has been his lifelong obsession. Now, it's given him a life."

Jack Lessenberry, a reporter who has covered Kevorkian's exploits for years and who knows him socially as well as professionally, agrees. "After a lifetime of not succeeding at the things he's undertaken, he's finally found something that has brought him acclaim. His work is what he has in life," Lessenberry says.

Since attending medical school, where he photographed patients at the point of dying to show the changes in their retinas, Kevorkian has had a lifelong fascination with death. The only son of Armenian immigrants, he grew up with an interest in science that led him from an engineering course at the University of Michigan in Pontiac to medical school. From the start, he was interested in autopsies and studied their history back to ancient Greece. In 1952, he became an intern at the Henry Ford Hospital in Detroit, and in 1955, after a couple of years of military service, accepted a pathology residency at the University of Michigan in Pontiac. He took on, and left, almost a dozen pathology positions from the late 1950s until his retirement in 1982. (His critics say that he is suspect because he has only ever worked as a pathologist, never as a clinician, and has therefore never had *living* patients.) He has also written articles and hatched a number of highly unorthodox schemes involving dying people and cadavers. For example, in the early 1960s, he worked on a project at the Pontiac General Hospital transfusing the blood of dead people into the bodies of the living. "It's just a transplant! Blood is an organ! A liquid organ," the doctor explained to a dubious reporter. "After all, the Russians had been doing it clinically for over forty years." But an application for a federal grant to continue his research on battlefields—specifically, under combat conditions in Vietnam—was turned down.

In the late 1970s and early 1980s, Kevorkian turned his mind to another controversial scheme: persuading prisoners on death row to donate their organs for transplant on their execution. He took his idea to various legislative and congressional committees, and even obtained written consent from a few condemned prisoners. But no one was prepared to implement the plan, and it was roundly criticized in the medical press for its outlandish nature. In his book, *Prescription: Medicide, The Goodness of Planned Death,* Kevorkian outlines the scheme and writes about his increasing cynicism and bitterness with the timidity of the authorities. "I resolved never again to waste time and effort in futile appeals for support from government agencies," he says.

To critics of his projects, Kevorkian explains that he is simply not awed by the so-called sanctity of the human body; instead, he's fascinated to contemplate what the dead can offer the living in terms of medical research and harvested organs. Indeed, donating the organs from people he helps to die is still part of his declared plan.

According to his supporters, Kevorkian is a clever and cultivated man, a church organist and flute player who declares a passion for Bach, and composes his own music. He is also a painter, and has created some extremely disturbing art works: huge, somber canvases, with gruesome images of death and destruction in stark, uncluttered forms, dripping blood and guts. (The frames of two of his paintings are stained with his own blood.) At one time, Fieger asked him to sell some of his works to raise money for his cause, but Kevorkian refused. When asked why, he is reported to have said, "Would you sell one of your children?"

The physician is renowned for his complete lack of interest in material things. He never accepts money for his work and says that, when he finishes with it, he plans to dismantle the van in which he has carried out many of his suicides, so that no one will be able to exploit it for financial gain. However, in 1997, he produced a compact disk of original jazz music, featuring himself playing flute, backed by a group of musicians called the Morpheus Quartet. The disk itself is mischievously entitled "A Very Still Life: the Kevorkian Suite," and $4 of its $18.98 price is donated to Kevorkian's efforts to open an assisted suicide clinic.

Kevorkian first became caught up in the subject of assisted death in 1989 when he heard about the plight of 38-year-old David Rivlin, who at age 19 had been rendered a quadriplegic in a surfing accident, and now, almost entirely paralyzed and on a respirator, was making a plea to the courts to be allowed to die. When the judge agreed, Rivlin became the first person in modern history to be given permission to end his life.

During Rivlin's hearing, Kevorkian, who had by then retired from pathology and was putting his energies into sub-
mitting articles to medical journals (most of which were
turned down), occupied himself with the challenge of how
Rivlin would die. With parts collected from junk shops and
street fairs, Kevorkian jerry-rigged a "death machine" (which
he initially called a Thanatron until his lawyer suggested
that Mercitron might have a more humane ring) that could
deliver a fatal dose of potassium chloride through an intravenous line attached to the patient's arm, with just one easy
flick of a switch. The idea was for an incapacitated patient
like Rivlin to be able to activate the switch himself, thus
making his death officially a suicide. In the end, Rivlin chose
to die in a hospice, tranquilized to unconsciousness while his
respirator was removed. But for Kevorkian, there was no
turning back: He informed the public of the existence of his
suicide machine, and of his determination to put it to use.
People from around the country began to respond.

The first person to use the Mercitron was Janet Adkins,
a 54-year-old woman from Portland, Oregon. Adkins was in
the early stages of Alzheimer's disease, and desperate to kill
herself before she became incapable of carrying it out.
Kevorkian was wary of her at the start; he has admitted that
he knew Adkins was the wrong person to begin with, as she
was not suffering from terminal cancer. What's more, having
been turned away from a number of motels, private homes,
y office spaces, and funeral parlors, Kevorkian was
to help her die in the back of his Volkswagen van—an-

other move that he knew would evoke harsh criticism. Yet he agreed to perform Adkins's request, he said, because she was so distraught. "I decided I had to do it anyway," he said. "For the patient. That's what a real physician is for. To hell with the goddanged ethicists. I'm a *real* physician."

"People criticize him for doing it in a rusty old van, but it's society that's made it happen this way," said his close friend, Janet Good. "Anyway, it's not a rusty old van—it's old but it's immaculate inside. Jack always says when a baby is born in a rusty old taxi, people think it's great. But they don't use the same excitement when it comes to someone dying that way."

In 1991, Kevorkian was arrested for his role in Adkins's death, and he faced what would be the first of four jury trials for assisting a death. (In the Adkins trial, he was actually charged with murder.) Although juries have three times refused to indict him, local judges have not been so forgiving. The homicide charges against him were dropped, but his medical license was suspended in both Michigan and California, and his Mercitron was taken away. Kevorkian had by this time worked out a way to keep helping his so-called patients, even without a license: He could rig up a contraption using a canister of carbon monoxide gas and a mask; he wouldn't need a prescription to get either of those. And he had been told in medical school that carbon monoxide was the best way to commit suicide. He said that it gave a dead body a "rosy glow."

More charges were brought against Kevorkian in the autumn of 1996. Prosecutors in two separate states accused him of having reverted from using carbon monoxide to implementing a suicide contraption, delivering two separate medications via injection: sodium pentothal to render the patient unconscious and potassium chloride to stop the heart. As well as working with medications that he was no longer licensed to use, Kevorkian has developed other signs of recklessness. During the early days, he would call police after a death had taken place to come and pick up the body: more recently, he has started taking the body to an area hospital, because, he says, he wants to allow the family to grieve, uninterrupted by the arrival of police, and also to spare them the trauma of watching news footage of their loved one being carried off in a body bag. Prosecutors say the physician knows that moving a body after a death is a felony.

Kevorkian has three things going for him that have so far kept him out of prison: a sloppy, ill-defined state law governing assisted suicide; the widespread support of the public, which has resulted in three different juries finding him not guilty at his trials; and perhaps most important, his lawyer, Geoffrey Fieger.

Forty-seven-year-old Fieger, a flamboyant, larger-than-life individual, inherited his father's law firm and has turned it into a highly lucrative practice specializing in medical malpractice and personal injury. He takes high-profile, big-money cases and defends them aggressively, theatrically, and successfully. He was probably a millionaire before Kevorkian made him a star. Now, he's something of a celebrity and very rich indeed: In 1993 alone, he won an $18 million judgment. He owns five homes, one in the Caribbean, and one that he rents to Kevorkian for just $350 a month. He lives well, vacations in style, dines at Detroit's finest restaurants, and until now, has defended Kevorkian for free.

Fieger and Kevorkian—Geoff and Jack, as the local press calls them—make a fascinating pair: Fieger is burly, cocksure, and sophisticated, a verbal bullyboy with an undeniable gift of the gab; he is ruthless and crude, rumored to threaten his opponents with personal ruin and call them all manner of names, from "asshole" to "imbecile." Meanwhile, Kevorkian is bony, impolitic, and guileless to a fault. Together, they are a modern Don Quixote and Sancho Panza— except that the windmills at which they're tilting are real. Where Kevorkian faces the world with his blunt conviction that what he does is right, Fieger dances with logic and the law, dazzling with words, fencing with the truth, performing to the gallery with an unflinching confidence in his ability to sweep away all of the delicate shadings that give the right-to-die issue such depth and complexity.

"This isn't about shades of gray, it's simple, it's black and white," Fieger booms across a conference hall full of rapt admirers. And for the length of his speech, it *is* simple. "If committing suicide is a legal act, how can assisting a legal act be an *illegal* act?" he asks. And for a moment, you agree: Simple, logical. A perfect example of Fieger's evangelical sophistry.

Yet the lawyer isn't always delicate. In 1997, he was fined $7500 for trying to influence the outcome of a court hearing by angling to get a particular judge. 1997 was also the year that Fieger managed to get Kevorkian's fourth, and potentially least winnable, case dismissed from court by breaking so many rules in his opening arguments that the judge declared a mistrial.

It will be interesting to see whether, faced with any further legal action, Fieger's partner, Michael Schwartz, will be as effective in keeping the renegade physician out of trouble. In January 1998, Fieger announced his decision to step aside as Kevorkian's defender in order to run for political office, that of governor of Michigan, against the three-time incumbent, John Engler. Fieger has said that he will allot at least $1 million of his own money to his campaign.

Although Kevorkian has always been portrayed by the media as a lone figure battling his way unaided, Fieger is just one of a loyal group of people who have been involved with Kevorkian's activities over the years.

To begin with, there was only his sister, Margo Janus, who acted as his unofficial assistant, chauffeuring clients to him and liaising with their families, until her sudden death of a heart attack in 1994. Other assistants have included Neil Nicol, a medical supplies salesman who has worked with the physician for years, and Georges Reding, a psychiatrist who helps him establish the mental competence of his patients. Reding is one of six Michigan physicians who, in October 1995, formed a group called "Physicians for Mercy." Their stated aim is to ensure that "qualified medical personnel should be able to assist adult, competent human beings to terminate their suffering, under appropriate circumstances, by assisting in the ending of life." Witnesses say that at least one and sometimes more members of the group are usually present when a death takes place. Reding is the only one who announces his presence at the deathbeds. In recent months, he has chosen to make his role more conspicuous, admitting, with increasing regularity, his involvement with the Kevorkian deaths, and speaking out in defense of his actions. Curiously, Reding remains a fairly unknown figure, spared so far from the intense scrutiny that his famous associate has undergone. To begin with, critics quickly went to work to discredit Reding, digging up controversies about his past career and writing him off as an unethical crank. Reding belongs to a group of psychiatrists who do not believe in institutionalizing people for mental illness. But while some of his former colleagues were quick to denounce his methods as unprincipled and bizarre, others have testified to his brilliance and humanity, and after an initial flurry of interest, the press has largely chosen to leave him alone. As for Reding himself, the Belgian-born physician told reporters that he was "embarrassed by the cowardice of my profession" in not supporting Kevorkian's work, and has made it clear that he plans to continue actively supporting it. "We are learning to die from our patients," Reding has said. "Not one has shown any sign of fear."

In recent years, there has also been one prominent woman involved in Kevorkian's activites: Janet Good. Good, a longtime right-to-die activist who started one of the earliest Hemlock Society chapters in Michigan back in 1989, stepped in to more or less fill the spot left vacant by Janus's death. And until her own death in August 1997 at the age of 73, Good became Kevorkian's most visible collaborator.

Good's unswerving devotion to Kevorkian helped him in several ways. First, her respectable, grandmotherly brand of compassion softened the image of Kevorkian's outlandishness, which persisted despite her insistence that he was "one of the kindest, most cultured and most compassionate men ever born." Good was a well-respected local figure, with a distinguished career as an equal opportunities official for the state government, a Girl Scout leader, and founder of, as well as campaigner for, numerous feminist groups and causes. For her accomplishments she was inducted into the Michigan Women's Hall of Fame in 1991. Furthermore, Good brought the physician into the computer age: She corresponded with and selected potential "patients" from the Internet. Then she sat with them when their deaths took place (although she always refused to say in what capacity) and in some cases, made lasting friendships with their families. "I feel so good helping people out of their agony," she told me shortly before her death. "I stay with them when they die and they hold my hand and say, 'Thank you, thank you.' I'm so at peace with myself knowing that I have enough courage to do this. I feel proud of myself to know that I wasn't afraid, proud that I knew what was right."

At the final stages of her own 2½-year struggle with cancer, Good had hospice care, but finally, it was Kevorkian who helped Good to die. Once again, coroner Dragovic announced at her autopsy that, although signs of her cancer were present, there was no evidence that the disease had reached its end stage. Dragovic classified her death—as he has classified those of all the Kevorkian "patients" he has autopsied—a homicide.

For all of his apparent bloodlessness, Kevorkian is a figure who can inspire passion in others. He inspired it in Good, who spoke worshipfully of him at all times, and he has inspired it in numerous others. And although he has been single and unattached all of his life, Kevorkian has admitted that he regrets never having married. He is said to be quite flirtatious, and to enjoy the company of women. He drew considerable attention when he turned up at *Time* magazine's 75th birthday party in New York City in March 1998 with a glamorous ("Drop-Dead Gorgeous," as some newspapers put it) 32-year-old attorney on his arm—a lawyer at Fieger's law firm of Fieger, Fieger and Schwartz—and conspicuously stroked her bare arms and back. Critics who note that his patient roster has consisted of far more women than men claim to see in this a scary kind of misogyny. Between 1990 and 1998, 55 of 76 known patients were women. But this dark claim is another that his supporters vigorously deny.

Kevorkian himself says that women seek out his services in greater numbers than men because women are more in tune with nature, more practical, and more ready to face suicide than men are. Reporter Jack Lessenberry says that, unlike men, who are more likely to go off on their own and shoot themselves, women's need for support during their final act is what brings them to Kevorkian. When they come to him, they are rewarded by his sympathy and attention. "This is where he functions most fully as a physician—in the time he gives these dying women," Lessenberry says.

However, research by two leading experts in the field of suicide has reached more worrisome conclusions. An ongoing study at Columbia–Michael Reese Hospital in Chicago suggests that the women who approach Kevorkian may be acting out of depression and hopelessness. The study's main author, Kalman J. Kaplan, explains: "Women especially feel they have no right to get help, and feel they are only of worth when they are healthy and not ill." As a result, he says, when they are diagnosed with a chronic illness, they feel they owe it to their families not to be a burden, but to quickly get out of the way.

The American Association of Suicidology, which has also speculated on why Kevorkian's "patient" list has included such a preponderance of women (68 percent of 40 cases that they studied), reached similar conclusions. Noting that fewer of the women than the men who came to Kevorkian were officially deemed "terminally ill," the report concludes: "Many of these women may have been considering suicide for psycho-social rather than medical reasons. . . . Rather than dissuade his patients in their attempt at suicide, Kevorkian helps them carry out plans about which they may be initially ambivalent."

Critics fear that ambivalence may be just one of several emotions Kevorkian is not prepared to acknowledge. What they fear—with men as well as women—is that among those he chooses to "help" may be people too mentally unbalanced to make a rational decision about hastening their death, or those who might change their minds, or even lose control during the dying process. Reporter Betzold, author of *Appointment with Dr. Death,* has written that over the years, "Kevorkian's 'medical service' has been rife with crucial questions about the hidden issues in assisted suicide. . . . The irony of Kevorkian is that Americans frightened of dying and mistrustful of physicians have been sold on a plan to give physicians much greater power to decide who lives and who dies. A medical maverick has paved the way for total physician control over life and death."

To begin with, many right-to-die advocates, mindful of Kevorkian's role as the lightning conductor of their cause, tried to tiptoe around the "Kevorkian issue," careful not to criticize him openly.

"Kevorkian has posed a 'challenge' to the movement," said Choice in Dying's Mary Mayer, in the kind of diplomatic doublespeak usually reserved for Washington politicians. "He has raised the issue of how much suffering isn't being addressed by physicians and palliative care. Many people feel the medical profession has failed them, and Kevorkian hasn't. But," she adds, "people must be made to realize that there's a middle ground between Kevorkian and suffering."

Over time, a growing number of campaigners have become more outspoken in their public comments. Kathryn L. Tucker, the attorney who presented the case for assisted dying before the Supreme Court, has publicly referred to Kevorkian as a "backstreet provider" (prompting his lawyer, Fieger, to admonish her for creating "internecine warfare" among supposed allies). And in a *New York Times* editorial that ran in the summer of 1996, two leading movement "moderates," journalist Betty Rollin, who wrote the moving book *Last Wish,* about her own experiences helping her terminally ill mother to die, and physician Timothy Quill, who has admitted assisting in at least one of his own patients' deaths, called Kevorkian "on a rampage" and "out of control." Quill is one of the few who has been publicly critical of Kevorkian's methods from the start, and has long considered his actions to be both scary and provocative.

"He has deeply frightened us by the ease with which he helps patients to die, and by his apparent lack of doubt, uncertainty, or careful analysis of his patients and their problems," Quill wrote in his 1993 book, *Death and Dignity: Making Choices and Taking Charge.* "He appears more interested in challenging society and the medical profession than in engaging with individual dying patients in their struggle to find their own path."

Kevorkian might argue that there is nothing wrong with such ambitions: He feels his entire professional life has been spent challenging what he sees as the cowardice of society and the medical profession. He is not about conciliation;

that's something he leaves to the right-to-die groups that he openly disdains for being prepared only to talk the talk, not walk the walk, as he alone has done. His particular dislike of Derek Humphry, for example, whom he denounces for not being a physician and for not actually helping people die, is of long standing. In 1980, at the very start of the movement, Humphry refused to publish Kevorkian's articles in the Hemlock Society journals because they seemed too radical. The two now keep a cool distance, although Humphry emphasizes that he has nothing personally against Kevorkian, and he is careful to acknowledge the physician's role in helping the movement gain national attention. "Kevorkian's on a mission against organized medicine," says Humphry. "But we're into changing the laws."

So is the Michigan legislature. Kevorkian's own lawmakers, surely embarrassed at their almost decade-long impotence to stop his activities, remain hellbent on revenge and have made it clear they will not let up until Kevorkian is put out of business. In early January 1998, during an unannounced, late-night session, local politicians speedily signed into power a Michigan Death with Dignity Act, designed to impose a watertight common-law ban on physician-assisted death. State senator William Van Regenmorter, a fervent Kevorkian opponent, has launched a second bill through the senate calling for an outright ban on assisted suicide.

Meanwhile, Kevorkian remains secure in his public support, and seemingly oblivious to the larger canvas taking shape around him. In 1997, while the Supreme Court, numerous state legislatures and professional organizations were augustly weighing the complexities of assisted death, Kevorkian continued to forge ahead on his own crusade, apparently unperturbed by either literal or legal subtleties.

On the other hand, the mainstream organizations are acutely aware of him, and his continued operations give all sides of the debate added fuel. Opponents of physician-assisted dying point to them as proof of how anarchically the procedure would work if it were legalized, and how the country, like the man himself, would soon move on from helping just the terminally physically ill to die to those with chronic diseases or histories of mental suffering. Even those who support Kevorkian's work in principle can point to his unorthodox choices to make the case for needing laws, to bring the practice under tighter control.

Whatever the outcome in Michigan, one thing remains sure: Kevorkian will not be giving up his operations anytime soon. And if he is forced to, he will not go quietly. He has sworn to continue fighting for his cause—if need be, to the death. Nobody doubts that he will.

♦ **CHAPTER 7** ♦

The Leading Activists
and Their Obsessive
Quest

Action will furnish belief—but will
that belief be the true one?
          —Arthur Hugh Clough

Jack Kevorkian may be the most famous right-to-die activist in the world, but he is far from being the only one—or the first. A full decade before Dr. K. and his suicide machine emerged from the heartland, a British-born activist, Derek Humphry, had launched America's first grass-roots right-to-die organization, and was encouraging its still-timid members to ignite the sparks of what was to become a fiery national debate.

The 68-year-old Humphry is everything Kevorkian is not: political, polished, and adept with words and social situations. Kevorkian won't leave his home base, but Humphry flies all over the world, and clearly enjoys the networking, the conferences, and the attention. And although he has choen a very different manner of promoting his cause, his personal life has, in dramatic ways, been more closely colored by his unusual calling than Kevorkian's has.

Today, Humphry, the founding father of the Hemlock Society, who retired in 1992 after 12 years as executive director, has become a kind of roving éminence grise of the movement, a respected elder statesman whose place in the annals of the crusade is assured, and earned.

"For most of us, Derek Humphry is where it all began," said fellow activist, Janet Good.

Humphry is a walking encyclopedia of deathlore, steeped in history, law, lethal doses, and other foolproof suicide methods, such as the notorious Hemlock trademark technique of placing a plastic bag over the head to ensure certain death. He is generous in sharing his knowledge with fellow supporters, journalists, and students alike. In the 1970s, he was a journalist with the London *Sunday Times*, and I knew him then. For a year or so, we were both reporting race relations, at a time when they were becoming sour in Britain. We would frequently show up to cover the same events for our respective newspapers. He was courteous and helpful, and I had absolutely no inkling that one day he would become a subject of my work.

In 1980, when Humphry and his second wife, Ann Wickett, started the Hemlock Society in Los Angeles, there were already a few American right-to-die societies in existence. But these were moderate, modeled after the early British euthanasia societies, and concerned mainly with raising public awareness and promoting living wills. The group Humphry wanted to start was different. It came into being on the coat-tails of his personal admission, in his book *Jean's Way,* that he had helped his fatally ill first wife to die a few years ear-lier. Hemlock's stated goal was to establish people's right to seek physician-assisted suicide.

Based on the organization's current success, it is hard to imagine that in those early days, Hemlock's members, pio-neers in the field of death and dying, were fighting a national trend of denial and deaf ears. "For the first five years, I was very much alone," Humphry says. "It was the hardest job in the world selling death—albeit a good death. Just getting a paragraph in a newspaper was incredibly exciting."

By the late 1980s and early 1990s, Humphry's profile had risen considerably. He crisscrossed the country giving speeches and attending conferences. He wrote editorials in the local Oregon press and from time to time, in national newspapers like the *New York Times.* He financed Hemlock activities from the proceeds of his books, and was everyone's favorite spokesperson on death and dying, always willing and knowledgeable, sometimes outspoken and provocative.

Despite his apparently unchallenged authority, Hum-phry has had his bumpy times in the movement. There are some who consider him too radical and too outspoken at the wrong times. Shortly before the vote on Oregon's Measure 16, for example, Humphry told local reporters that he didn't think the measure went far enough, and should also include voluntary euthanasia. Although the measure succeeded, the

51 to 49 percent margin was uncomfortably close, and some activists blamed Humphry for having turned off the all-important "undecided" voters, just 2 percent of whom could have changed the outcome.

More alarming, though, is that his private life has been touched by the kind of scandal that the movement is all too anxious to avoid. His personal problems have spilled messily out into the open. "Given the nature of his problems, he hasn't helped our credibility," commented one of Humphry's critics.

The trouble began in 1989, when he left his second wife, Ann Wickett, shortly after she had undergone a mastectomy for breast cancer. Wickett had written a book, *Double Exit,* which was published that year. The book told how Wickett and Humphry had helped Wickett's parents to die in a suicide pact. But in the book, Wickett revealed that while her 92-year-old father was ready to die, her 78-year-old mother had not been. In the midst of her suicide, Wickett recounted, she seemed to change her mind, and Wickett ended up having to restrain her as she died. It was a messy and unhappy conclusion that haunted her daughter afterward. One day, in the midst of Humphry and Wickett's equally messy divorce proceedings, Humphry left an angry message on his ex-wife's answering machine threatening to expose her role in her mother's death if she didn't leave him alone.

Two years later, having survived her cancer but succumbed to despair over Humphry's desertion, Wickett committed suicide. She rode a horse deep into the Oregon wilderness, took a fatal dose of drugs, and lay down under a tree to die. It took rescue workers days to find her body, but the suicide note Wickett had left behind was more quickly discovered and leaked to the press.

The letter unequivocally blamed Humphry for her death.

"There. You got what you wanted. Ever since I was diagnosed as having cancer, you have done everything conceivable to precipitate my death," the letter said.

"I was not alone in recognizing what you were doing. What you did—desertion and abandonment and subsequent harassment of a dying woman—is so unspeakable there are no words to describe the horror of it. Yet you know. And others know too. You will have to live with this until you die. May you never, ever forget."

Wickett left a copy of the note for Rita Marker, an antieuthanasia activist who had become a close friend of hers, and to whom she had written a postscript. It said: "Rita: My final words to Derek. He is a killer. *I know.* Jean actually died of suffocation. I could never say it until now; who would believe me? Do the best you can. Ann."

It seemed as if the scandal of Ann Wickett's death might engulf Humphry; the press descended in force. One journalist who turned up to pick over the bones was Cal McCrystal, a former colleague from Humphry's reporter days at the *Sunday Times.* McCrystal wrote a scathing article about Humphry in *Vanity Fair,* accusing him, among other things, of "earnest, unapologetic self-centeredness."

Humphry remembers that McCrystal, who had been his editor back in London, had never liked him and now relished the opportunity to stick a journalistic knife into his back. Still, the damage was done—to the degree that Humphry felt the need to take out a half-page advertisement in the *New York Times* to dispel rumors of his moral culpability. Ann, he wrote, at times had depressions "so serious that she had to be hospitalized." The advertisement went on to say that Hemlock did not support the idea of "suicide for reasons of depression."

Five years later, when he and I met again at the Hemlock Society conference in Denver, Humphry spoke openly about his years with Wickett. I had not been looking forward to raising the subject, but he brought the subject up himself, offering information freely. He recalled the years after his breakup with Ann and before her death as distressing, difficult, and plagued by the fear that she would do something harmful to either him or herself—as she did. But Humphry claims that the accusations against him were deeply hurtful and untrue. He describes Ann as a beautiful, brilliant, and severely troubled woman. "I should have recognized how troubled she was before I married her," he says now. "Others in the movement knew she had problems. Unfortunately, I didn't find out until too late."

He is still upset about Ann's accusation that he suffocated Jean. "She knew I didn't do that to Jean," he said. "She wrote the book with me. She knew exactly what happened."

Today, the scandal still lingers. In 1997, a British television company broadcast a drama supposedly based on his life story, called *Goodbye My Love* (the final words he said to Jean). The company neither approached Humphry for his cooperation nor did they let him see the finished product before they aired it. Humphry, who has since seen it, says 25 percent of it is total fabrication, and he obviously hopes it will not reignite extinguished flames.

In the meantime, he appears to have ridden out the tough times. He resigned his position as Hemlock leader in 1992, largely, he maintains, because he had become burned-out and felt the movement needed some fresh energy at its helm. Insiders say he really stepped down for the good of the cause, realizing how potentially damaging his presence had come to be. Whatever the reasons, Humphry has proved himself to be a survivor: He has remarried and retreated to the hills behind Eugene, Oregon, where he lives with his third wife, Gretchen. He spends his days running his own smaller-scale, research-based organization, ERGO! the Euthanasia Research and Guidance Organization, and makes his living writing books and articles. He continues to make himself available to answer questions and make occasional public appearances. And, occasionally, he admits, he also gives out "self-deliverance" advice to desperate callers over the telephone. An updated version of *Final Exit,* with lists of new drugs and more foolproof methods of "self-deliverance," as well as a history of his involvement with the movement, was published in 1997.

We will probably never know what really happened between Derek Humphry and Ann Wickett, but there is no doubt that it's uncomfortable for this movement concerned with death to contain a man who has been involved in assisting at the deaths of at least three people close to him. (He also "pulled the plug" on his brother, left brain dead after a serious illness.)

To those of us looking on, Humphry's 20 years in the movement might indicate a peculiar obsession, a bizarre preoccupation with death. That same quality is present in Kevorkian, Australian physician Philip Nitschke, Canadian activist John Hofsess, and other key members of the right-to-die movement worldwide. Does their commitment qualify as an obsession? Or is it no more than the intense involvement of a stock trader or a politician, whose thirst for risk, control, or power strikes no one as especially strange. Certainly, helping a desperately ill loved one to die may feed a person's sense of both virtue and power, and defying the law to do so may cause a rush of danger, a thrill of risk. The leaders of the Death with Dignity crusade feel that they must keep intervening to perform this solemn human service, as all too few others are prepared to do the same. But all insist that there is nothing macabre or obsessive about it, that it is simply a compassionate response to a suffering human being.

"I've always been something of a campaigner, trying to turn my abilities toward injustice and reform," Humphry says. "When you see someone you love suffering abysmally in front of you, the law flies out of the window. You say, 'I've got to do what I've got to do.' As a humanitarian, I'm willing to buck the system and fight for the law reform that I believe is right. And I shall carry on until the fight is won, or until I drop dead." One hesitates to ask him how.

But Philip Nitschke, Australia's foremost right-to-die advocate, is not planning to stick around that long. He has been beaten down by the ferocity of the opposition, and he wants out from under the klieg lights—as soon as possible.

Nitschke, 50, is a forthright, blunt-talking man of action, as free-spirited as the wide-open land on which he lives and works. A former forest ranger who was forced to retire because of a foot injury, Nitschke came to medicine at the relatively advanced age of 43. Initially, he worked with drug addicts and prostitutes—"a sort of wretched-of-the-earth kind of practice," as he describes it—and fought an unsuccessful battle with local authorities in his home outside Darwin to open a methadone clinic for heroin addicts.

Nitschke's entry into the assisted-death debate was unplanned, he insists. When the Northern Territory's premier, Marshall Perron, launched the campaign, opponents insisted that physicians would never lend their support to such a law. "That's when I got involved," Nitschke says. "I thought, 'That's rubbish—I, for one, have always supported euthanasia,' and so I got together 20 physicians and we took out a full page ad in the local press saying, Look, there *is* enough support to pass this."

The legislation passed in parliament in the spring of 1995, and came into effect on July 1, 1996. Within that year, a number of terminally ill people, thinking the law was already active, arrived in the Territory, hoping to get help in dying from a local physician. Nitschke became involved with them and in several cases, fought for their right to die. "It was hard not to become associated with people's individual plights," he says. "How can one not want to help people who are suffering with dreadful terminal diseases?" One such individual, a retired cab driver named Max Bell, who was in the painful final stages of cancer, drove almost 2000 miles across country from New South Wales for Nitschke's aid— only to have to turn around and return home after learning that assisted death was still illegal.

After the law came into force, however, Nitschke came into his own as the central figure—the only figure—involved in orchestrating the deaths of the world's first three people to be legally helped to die. Along with computer programmer and associate Des Carne, Nitschke also devised the computer program that caused the three deaths. When the law was repealed a brief 9 months later, leaving two terminal patients frustrated at the verge of death, Nitschke put one of them, Esther Wilde, into a coma at her request, and kept her heavily sedated with increasing doses of drugs until she died 4 days later. Nitschke was furious that this particular act was still legal, while helping a patient to die no longer was.

Deliverance, the computer program designed by Nitschke for his patients, is an interactive software application that can be installed into any computer. The equipment must be hooked up to three syringes, each of which contains one of a fatal trio of drugs. The syringes are then inserted into the patient's veins. When the patient is ready, he or she reads the computer screen, which will successively display three questions. Each asks, in a different way, whether the patient is willing to proceed. "Are you certain you understand that if you proceed and press the YES button on the next screen that you will die?" the penultimate question asks. When the patient has indicated "Yes" for the third time, the computer activates a compressor through which the syringes administer their deadly medicine: first thiopentone sodium, then pentobarbitone sodium, and finally pancuronium.

Having successfully used this program on three patients, Nitschke was also planning to develop an alternative machine that would use carbon monoxide and an oxygen mask to help people die—a "slicker" version, as he describes it, of Kevorkian's Mercitron.

"When people get too old and frail it can be very difficult to get access to veins, and gas is a much easier way to go. Carbon monoxide is a painless and acceptable way," he explains. In recent months, Nitschke has also been developing a "suicide pill" made from nonprescription products available at drugstores or supermarkets that would enable "everyone who wishes to go down that path." He believes everyone should have the same access to lethal products as physicians do.

Nitschke has shown the same spirit of philanthropy with his Deliverance computer program, which he made available to others at his website as freeware, "to allow other developers to modify the program." He wanted to demystify the idea of "computer death," he said, so that eventually, a dying person would be able to control his or her own death without the physician having to be present—which Nitschke thinks patients and their families will ultimately prefer. As for the idea of making the computer a lethal weapon, he knows it could exacerbate some people's anxieties about computers, "but," he adds, "the people who are in favor of assisted suicide like it immensely."

Nitschke has a shrewd eye for the uses he can make of new technology. Sick of being pilloried in a predominantly hostile national press, he has decided to challenge the media at their own game. When the third terminally ill patient—a 69-year-old man with cancer—died under his care in early 1997, Nitschke chose not to inform the press in the traditional way, by holding a press conference. Instead, he posted a brief bulletin about the event, without even naming the patient, on his Deliverance homepage on the Internet. Word got out quickly; within 48 hours, almost 4000 people had logged on to the website to read the information. But it took a local reporter to understand the full significance of Nitschke's action. The reporter, Jon Casimir, wrote in Melbourne's *The Age* that by using the Internet, Nitschke was avoiding the inevitable bombardment of reporters' questions, and consequently, as he saw it, the manipulation of his words to fit someone else's interpretation of his motives. "The media is no longer something that is done to him, it is now something that he does," Casimir noted, commenting that this was also the first time in Australia that the Internet had been used to break a major news story.

But despite winning numerous battles, Nitschke has always had a disheartened feeling that he was losing the war.

From the start, he was pessimistic that the Northern Territory law would be overturned, and when it was, in March 1997, he could not hide his anger and disappointment. He decided at the time to withdraw from the center of the medical firestorm, a place he has said he hates to be. "Even though I get a lot of support from the community, I get a hell of a lot of criticism from within the profession," he says. "One feels one's professional isolation a great deal. The degree of ostracism has been hard."

Defeated and despondent, Nitschke told me at the time that he was ready to find someone to take over his leadership role. "It can't be just one person, and I'm tired," he said. "It has been a bitter, savage, and debilitating campaign on a political and personal level, and it's had significant personal costs. The deaths are extremely harrowing. You get to live with these people, to know them quite well and share the highs and lows of the process with them. Going through all that, and then helping them to die, takes its toll."

Nevertheless, a year after making this statement, Nitschke is still involved with Australia's right-to-die movement, and shows every sign of being in it for the long haul. He says his goals are now to unite the country in a demand for action. "Until now, the movement has been very fragmented. There are a number of state-based organizations but no federal coordinating body," he explains. "We've had trouble making the other states believe that the fate of one affects them all. But I think it's crucial to how this thing progresses in Australia in the future." A number of different

legislators around the country are currently engaged in getting an assisted dying law reinstated, and he has said that he
will move wherever such a law gets adopted, in order to continue his work. Whether or not he wants to walk away,
Nitschke seems to realize that his journey is not yet done.

For journalist and filmmaker John Hofsess, involvement
with the Canadian Right-to-Die Society has also been something of a rocky road. Ironically, his decision to start up the
society back in 1991 was more intellectual than emotional
when he made it. The invitation to start a Canadian offshoot
of the Hemlock Society came from Derek Humphry at a time
when Hofsess was ready for something new. He decided to
give it a try.

At that time, Canada already had one euthanasia society, Death with Dignity, based in Toronto. But Hofsess, inspired by the waves of activism that were sweeping up the
West Coast to where he lived in Vancouver, wanted his organization to be everything Death with Dignity wasn't. "They
seemed content to endlessly talk about change," Hofsess said.
"We wanted to provoke change."

Hofsess's big opportunity came in 1992, when he took on
the case of Sue Rodriguez, a 34-year-old mother who was suffering from ALS and who was desperate to find a physician to
help her die before muscle wastage would cause her to choke
to death.

"Sue and I made a contract that she would get help in
dying if she would let me publicize her case," Hofsess says.

He had a clear idea of what he wanted the Rodriguez case to achieve.

"We wanted her story to be like a two-act play," he explains. "In the first act, she'd become very well known. In the second, she'd be actively helped to die—either by myself or someone within the society—in a completely open manner, so either charges would be brought and I'd be convicted or jailed, or I wouldn't be charged, but because I had been so open about it, the law would have been sorely tested in the process."

But Hofsess only stage-managed the first act of his play. "As she became more famous, people were drawn to Sue to promote their own agendas," he says. One of those was a New Democrat Party member of Parliament, Svend Robinson, a self-proclaimed right-to-die supporter and adviser to Hofsess's group. Robinson, according to Hofsess, overrode Rodriguez's and Hofsess's pact and made his own arrangements with her. These included ending her association with the Right-to-Die Society of Canada, and forbidding her from doing any more publicity for the cause. When the time came for Rodriguez's death, in February 1994, Robinson brought in a "mystery physician" whom he refused to identify, and portrayed himself in the role of the faithful friend in whose arms she died.

Hofsess notes, "Something that should have had considerable political and legal clout came to nothing. How could charges be brought against a 'mystery physician?'" He adds bitterly, "We were on a roll when the Rodriguez case began, momentum was building, and we had the makings of a winning team. Then Robinson grabbed the ball and fumbled it. This is a case where a personally ambitious politician betrayed the original purpose of the Rodriguez case and turned it into a mere publicity stunt."

Hofsess claims that since that time, the Canadian right-to-die movement has been in "political and legal limbo." He lists a number of subsequent disappointments: In 1995, a special seven-member Senate Committee on Euthanasia and Assisted Suicide voted not to change the status quo on assisted dying. This meant that a free vote on the issue, which the government had already promised, was indefinitely deferred. Another disappointment, for which Hofsess takes personal blame, was an unsuccessful 1994 Supreme Court appeal, where the cause was defeated in a 4 to 5 vote. "It was my fault for hiring an incompetent lawyer," Hofsess says in retrospect. "And I'm haunted by the thought that if we had had a better one, perhaps we might have prevailed."

Despite the setbacks, Hofsess continues to devote himself wholeheartedly to his cause. In 1995, along with Derek Humphry, he started the online service, DeathNet, which has now been visited some 300,000 times, and has won a number of computer industry awards as an outstanding website. Hofsess also runs a private mailing list on the Internet called "Nothing But The News," providing members with daily reports of right-to-die developments around the world. He is an impressive resource on the subject and is widely consulted. The day we spoke, he had been awake until 5 AM helping Noel Earley, a 48-year-old Rhode Island man dying of ALS, draft a letter to President Clinton, appealing for his support for a physician-hastened death. (Earley died a few days later, without a physician's intervention.)

One of Hofsess's most recent projects has been the launch of a publication series entitled *The Art and Science of Suicide.* Its subject matter is not the "how to" material of books like *Final Exit,* but rather innovative methods of bringing about death that would be easily available to people without a physician's prescription. Hofsess is working on these methods with Rob Neils, Ph.D., a clinical psychologist and president of the Washington-based Dying Well Network, Philip Nitschke in Australia, and retired physician Pieter Admiraal in the Netherlands.

"We are conceivably talking here of LEGAL substances that may well induce death faster and more efficiently than the classical method of massive overdose," Hofsess explained in an e-mail to potential contributors, appealing for suggestions. What they need, he says, are methods using inert or compressed gasses, such as those used in scuba diving. The group's most advanced invention to date is a so-called "autoanoxygenic debreather," a mask that extracts carbon dioxide from the closed air system, leaving only nitrogen and diminishing amounts of oxygen to be inhaled. Hofsess claims that with the debreather, death would result in 15 minutes. Experimentation with other substances also continues. The group is looking for naturally occurring poisons and venoms, such as the kind found in Japanese blowfish and certain kinds of snakes. "Needless to say, we are looking for individuals with an interest in the darker side of nature studies," Hofsess wrote. He believes that with so many suffering members, right-to-die advocates have nothing less than a "moral obligation" to investigate "new and realistic means" of death.

Perhaps Hofsess is eager to compensate for what he considers to be his lack of success in bringing dynamic change to Canada. "We've had this spotty kind of success—we've been on the verge of making things happen in Canada, but we haven't quite succeeded," he admits. One reason, he says, is because, unlike their neighbors across the border, too few Canadians are prepared to fight. "It's only when people get actively involved and cross the line that the momentum really gets going," he says. "A movement is only as active as its activists."

Hofsess takes his share of the blame for this. After 6 years at the helm of his organization, he believes his leadership has not inspired satisfactory results and he gives himself another year to make some significant difference. "I believe running a right-to-die organization is like being CEO of a major company, and if you don't deliver, it's part of your obligation to throw yourself off the board," he says.

At the same time, he adds, it's hard to walk away. "I do what I do often with a feeling that I am trapped," he wrote to me one morning in a private e-mail. "Each time I think of abandoning the thankless task of trying to change a federal law in Canada (that the government is determined NOT to see changed), I am drawn into the personal predicaments of our members and others, desperate for assistance of some kind. I often end up thinking: if I don't do this, who will? It's not easy to walk away from human suffering once you have been exposed to it. And so I continue—but with profound unease."

♦ CHAPTER 8 ♦

The Rank and File
Just Your Normal
Next-Door Neighbors

He that cuts off twenty years of life
cuts off so many years of fearing death.
—William Shakespeare

With its adjoining meeting rooms, overpriced gift shop, and parsley-garnished rubber-chicken lunches, the Red Lion Hotel on the outskirts of Denver is the typically characterless kind of place favored for midlevel corporate conventions. In early November 1996, it was the venue for the ninth National Hemlock Society conference, and an estimated 325 people made their way there for the 3-day event from all parts of the United States. Outside the hotel, the snow-covered peaks of the Rocky Mountains changed colors throughout the day—from purple in the early morning to orange under the setting sun—in a stunning display of nature's immutability. But inside the windowless conference rooms, the delegates were too busy with mortality to notice. There were people to catch up with, a packed agenda to get through, and a notable eagerness among the assembled crowd to discuss the topic of the day: Death.

Each morning, equipped with sharpened pencils and stuffed information packets, the audience settled into their seats long before the speakers had arrived. There were waved "hellos" across the spacious auditorium, the clinking of coffee cups, and, from here and there, the high-pitched whistling of an untuned hearing aid. Mostly, there was a palpable feeling of buoyancy: The cause of assisted death had had an extraordinary year and at this gathering, there was much to celebrate—the passage of supportive legislation both at home and abroad, the entry of the Supreme Court into the fray, and, above all, a newfound sense of political legitimacy. Suddenly, this group of activists, once dismissed as morbid crackpots, had moved boldly from the lunatic fringes into the mainstream. Dr. Kevorkian was on *Newsweek*'s list of the 25 most influential people of 1996, along with President Clinton and Tom Cruise; the stories of right-to-die battles had become regular Movie-of-the-Week TV fodder, and the Supreme Court, in anticipation of their debate, had received as many as 50 amicus, or "friend of the court," briefs from national organizations, with opinions pro and con. Even for the disciples of hastened death, the haste with which the issue had gathered momentum was greater than they could ever have anticipated. The conference members were aware that this was perhaps the peak moment in their campaign, and they were determined to revel in it.

This was certainly a far cry from the Society's modest beginnings back in 1983, in a drafty Unitarian Church on the outskirts of San Francisco. Writer Anne Fadiman was one of just two journalists to attend that early meeting. She described the naive zeal of those earliest crusaders:

"In that innocent, pre-Kevorkian era, the Hemlock members were already old, tired and none too healthy-looking, but the right-to-die movement was still young and pure," Fadiman reported. "The small audience of mostly female partisans huddled together in the front pews, umbrellas furled at their feet. This was a congregation far too decorous to shout, 'Hallelujah!' but a WASP susurration of assent swept through the nave of the church whenever one of the speakers formulated a particularly high-minded aphorism: 'Let us value the quality of life, not the quantity.' 'Suicide ends the living process; euthanasia ends the dying process.' The featured speaker was a professor of ethics who declared that although self-determination for the terminally ill was a praiseworthy cause—indeed, a sacred trust—the members of Hemlock must never compromise their moral probity by going too far."

Times had certainly changed. Although the majority of members at the Denver conference were still older than the average pro basketball team, there was also a strong showing of younger, politically savvy movers and shakers: physicians, hospice workers, nurses, lawyers, civil liberties advocates, ethicists, and religious leaders. None of them looked afraid of stirring a little controversy. The news that picketers had gathered outside the hotel caused an outbreak of self-important applause. Various prominent members would creep out of meetings to conduct TV interviews for local stations, while the speakers delivered messages that went far beyond high-minded aphorisms. Attorney Kathryn Tucker, who had won the Oregon right-to-die case for Compassion in Dying earlier in the year, explained how she planned to present her case before the chief justices. Two AIDS social workers spoke of their work in establishing a criterion for "Rational Suicide," and Derek Humphry addressed a standing-room-only debate on "How to Avoid a Botched Suicide Attempt." Was this the real issue that had enticed the rank and file to this event? The talk included specific, undisguised information about drug types and lethal doses. It also contained a number of details striking in their banality; for example, that the best time to schedule one's demise is on a Friday evening or a Saturday, to avoid the telephone ringing or a delivery person showing up unexpectedly at the door; and that one must swallow a fatal dose of pills as quickly as possible, to avoid falling asleep before they're all gone. The elderly members, in particular, took careful instruction. In the bathroom during the break, gray-haired ladies compared notes on their stockpiles of pharmaceuticals. "If I don't have enough barbiturates, would a handful of aspirin do the trick?" asked one woman anxiously.

The Hemlock Society's ability to offer its members "something for everyone"—from political action to meeting places for the rank and file to air their personal end-of-life anxieties—is what makes it unique among the many right-to-die organizations that have sprung into being over the past decade. For a start, Hemlock is the only organization with a grass-roots membership. In 1998, it was claiming 25,000 members in 82 chapters nationwide. Hemlock is also a political force. It was instrumental in the drafting of the groundbreaking state initiatives on the West Coast—in California in 1988 and 1992, in Washington in 1991, and in Oregon in 1994. With money raised from membership fees, donations, and sales of books such as *Final Exit,* Hemlock also donated large sums to their campaigns: So far, with contributions of almost $900,000, it has been far and away the single largest political benefactor. Without these funds, the initiatives would probably never have reached the ballot box. Hemlock has also contributed to Merian's Friends, a Michigan pressure group formed to get an assisted death bill onto Michigan's state ballot in November 1998.

In recent years, the Hemlock Society has become notably more involved in actively guiding people toward finding the help they want in death. It runs support groups for terminally ill members, and its newest project provides them with "agents" to convey their end-of-life wishes, in the event that they lose consciousness and are without loved ones to act for them. This is quite a change of direction. Back in 1993, the board was reluctant to get involved with individual cases on the grounds that being charged with civil disobedience might result in steep legal costs. But Ralph Mero, a Unitarian Universalist minister and a senior Hemlock member from Oregon, was so opposed to this policy that he resigned. Mero left

Hemlock to start up his own group, Compassion in Dying, the first not-for-profit organization staffed by trained volunteers, and aimed to help people achieve their personal goals of hastening a "death with dignity," regardless of the current state of the law. Of course, the group claims that what they do involves nothing illegal. "We don't prescribe drugs and we don't administer them," insists Barbara Coombs Lee, who succeeded Mero as CID's executive director in 1996, when the minister relocated to Massachusetts. But just what they do, and how much, is difficult to say, as the volunteers are discreet and closely guarded about the exact nature of their involvement. What they do admit is that they go to patients' bedsides to keep them company through the dying process. "A lot of people have a great fear of being alone when they die, especially if they have inadequate knowledge of how to kill themselves," explains Mero. To date, he estimates that CID representatives have been present at about 30 people's deaths. He says that he himself has attended 7.

Compassion in Dying has also extended its work into the legal field. It was Compassion in Dying, on behalf of one of its "clients," that orchestrated the 1995 Washington State court case that landed before the Second Court of Appeals and, later, the Supreme Court. And it was CID's executive director, Barbara Coombs Lee, who was a leading light in getting Oregon's assisted dying law drafted and adopted.

There are a number of reasons—beyond the medical imperatives such as overuse of technology and the reluctance of physicians to face "defeat" in the face of death—why the death-with-dignity organizations have made such headway in recent years. A set of social and political currents has been inexorably pushing people to confront the issue of death in a more direct and self-involved way. One example is the steady growth of the consumer movement since the 1960s and 1970s. Today, people have become astute medical consumers, and through the intensifying political debate on health care reform, they have become aware that medicine in the 1990s is a commodity, on sale to the highest bidder. It's also a fallible commodity, as more and more people are finding out in the courts. Shoddy medical practices, faulty medical devices, insufficiently tested drugs: the possibility for huge medical malpractice settlements has opened up the once unchallenged sanctuary of the medical establishment. Highly skilled malpractice lawyers and their newly wealthy litigants have shown the public not only that physicians are mere mortals, but also that consumers have rights: the right to choose a physician, the right to a second opinion, the right to sue for services poorly rendered, and, most recently, the right to refuse treatment. Now, they're demanding yet another right: the right to *more* treatments—in this case, final treatments.

At least a half of all consumers—women—have learned empowerment through the women's health movement, where they have fought for, and won, significant medical victories: the right to more natural forms of childbirth, fewer cesareans and hysterectomies, alternative approaches to menopause, and the battle to keep abortion a safe and legal constitutional right. But in their relationship with the medical profession, women have suffered a number of bitter losses too. They have fallen victim to unsafe pregnancy drugs such as DES, which left their daughters infertile and vulnerable to cancer, as well as to certain brands of interuterine contraceptive devices (for example, the Dalkon Shield), which caused serious, irreversible gynecological problems. Most recently, hundreds of thousands of women filed lawsuits challenging their physicians over the safety of their silicone breast implants, which they believe have produced devastating autoimmune diseases. Their physicians vehemently deny the link.

Not surprisingly, many women harbor a lingering distrust of the medical establishment. Now that the generation of so-called first-wave feminists is growing older and more prone to disease, they are likely to aggressively assert their resistance to a paternalistic medical profession telling them how they must die. And given that women still tend to outlive men, antagonism between patient and physician is likely to become more commonplace as women continue to age.

There is another notable, although smaller, cultural influence at work, especially on the West Coast. In California, Oregon, and Washington, the right-to-die movement has taken its most powerful hold—not just in ballot initiatives, but also because the region is home to the Death with Dignity Education Center (San Mateo, California), Compassion in Dying (Seattle, Washington), Americans for Death with Dignity (San Carlos, California), ERGO! (Eugene, Oregon), and Oregon Right to Die (Portland). (Choice in Dying, whose principal areas of concern are better end-of-life care and the promotion of living wills, is headquartered in New York. The Hemlock Society recently moved to Denver, but its roots are also firmly in the West.)

This is also the place where the New Age movement is most strongly rooted—a movement that flirts audaciously with death, enticing people to embrace "the life beyond" as never before in Western culture. Near-deathers, the growing movement of people who say they have been on the threshold of death but returned from it, describe dying as an alluring and transformational experience to be welcomed, not feared. For New Agers, it is the "ultimate trip," the climax of our spiritual journey. When New Age guru Timothy Leary became terminally ill and decided to play out his death on the Internet, literally thousands of curious people visited his homepage every day, until, shortly before his death, he finally "dropped out." Nonetheless, it was a timely cultural notion: the spirit released into cyberspace.

But there are also disturbing aspects to the New Agers' fascination with assisted suicide. Some feel that many of these New Age "death junkies' have drifted toward the death with dignity organizations, such as Hemlock and Compassion in Dying, to seek out the company of dying people for their own selfish motives: to kindle in themselves a sense of sanctity and intensity that only the solemnity of death can instill. In his book *A Chosen Death: The Dying Confront Assisted Suicide,* physician Lonnie Shavelson recounts a chilling story of a woman volunteer with a right-to-die organization who virtually kills a man she has offered to "help" die, in the hope of reliving the intensely loving experience that she had when, some time earlier, she had helped her desperately ill best friend to die. According to Herbert Hendin, executive director of the American Suicide Foundation, people's search for meaning in death—usually the death of others—is not new. "There is something about these people who say that the most moving experience of their life was helping someone to die. They say it's a closeness closer than any other bond. To me, there is something pathological about that."

From earliest times, people have been drawn to witness the experience of death. They've come out en masse to watch Christians being thrown to the lions, or common criminals being hanged in the town square, or the cleanly severed heads of the French bourgeoisie bounce off the guillotine. Kevorkian's particular fascination with the moment of dying has been discussed earlier in the book, as has that of certain European physicians and international activists. To a lesser degree, the full-time organizers of the right-to-die groups must also have a deeper level of interest in dying than the rest of us, for they choose to be immersed in the subject day after day.

Of course, most of these full-timers are immersed in far less existential aspects of the business, such as stuffing envelopes with political fliers or booking conference rooms. For some organizations, like Oregon Death with Dignity, the relationship with death was actually designed to be of a much more limited and pragmatic nature, namely, to pass ballot initiatives within that particular state. Other groups, like the Death with Dignity Education Center, keep a detachment through the distancing powers of intellectual debate. The DDEC organizes high-powered conferences and seminars that bring together the foremost thinkers in the different fields that converge within this debate: medicine, law, and ethics. Until recently, the meetings have taken place almost exclusively on the West Coast, where understanding of the issues is considered to be more highly evolved than in the rest of the country. But in November 1996, DDEC organized its first major East Coast conference under the beautiful arched ceilings of Manhattan's exclusive University Club.

The Center brought together an impressive array of experts who braved a New York rainstorm to deliver their opposing messages before a specially invited audience. Their arguments pro and con physician-assisted death were intellectually demanding and bolstered by slews of studies and statistics. The hours of debate, which continued through lunchtime and a snatched cup of afternoon tea, were intense and called for unflagging concentration. True, by the end of it, the East Coast audience could claim to have become more familiar with the profoundly complex issues at stake in this difficult controversy. Yet, in all of the hours of theory about law and language and the need for safeguards, there had been little evocation of the awesomeness of death within the context of real, suffering lives. There were no stories of the prolonged anguish of dying loved ones, no emotions on display under the lofty arches. Even *New England Journal of Medicine* executive editor Marcia Angell, one of the main speakers, chose to rebut a number of philosophical arguments before she confided to the audience that her own father, when diagnosed with a fatal cancer, had shot himself to death rather than enter the hospital and lose control over the remainder of his life.

For some right-to-die supporters, no matter what approach the organizations take, or what reform they try to achieve, they will always fall far short of expectations. One woman was furious that Compassion in Dying could provide her with neither a prescription for lethal drugs nor the name of a physician in her neighborhood who would write one for her—on demand. Another woman, the mother of a severely autistic child, came specifically to the society's Denver conference to address her concerns for her handicapped daughter, and other children like her. Many of these children are raised, she says, in deplorable conditions in state-run homes, where they never feel the sun on their faces and are left in wheelchairs for so long that their spines cave in. The woman says she has attended government meetings in her home state of Nebraska for years demanding changes, but claims that the legislature refuses to heed her arguments.

"The legislators asked me if I'd be prepared to mercy kill my daughter," she says, her eyes brimming with tears. "I tell them, the day that I die, I would prefer to kill her than let her live in neglect in a state-run home, because no one would care for her as I do."

Despite her evident passion, this woman found no one at the conference who responded to her words, and she left Denver feeling deeply disappointed that the organization's goals were not more far-reaching.

"I perceived Hemlock as the route to mercy killing to relieve suffering, but it turns out it's only for people who can consciously and willfully act to self-deliver, and I feel let down," this deceptively soft-spoken woman said. "If this were just the first step in a progressive movement, I'd stay. But this is a conspiracy of silence, and I won't renew my membership."

In many ways, this quiet, earnest mother of three is the right-to-die movement's worst nightmare—someone who poses some deeply uncomfortable issues for these organizations—issues that society may not yet, if ever, be ready to face. Her calls for death—no, euthanasia on demand—go way beyond those of the various right-to-die societies, all of which are intent on emphasizing that they do not want to put involuntary euthanasia on their agenda, or to make vulnerable members of society feel targeted by their demands. If any other supporters of physician-assisted death share such contentious views, they are very discreet about airing them. Rather, they are mindful of the fact that they have come a long way toward legalizing aid in dying, and they are anxious not to appear too far-out or extreme now.

Thus, members of the different right-to-die organizations work hard to show the public a united front, despite undoubted philosophical and personal rifts among them. One group finds the other too strident, or too cautious, or not outspoken enough. One believes that the way to get change is to empower people to take their end-of-life decisions into their own hands; the other argues that the only way to change society can be through the law.

On one issue all of the groups agree: that they can exert a subtle control over the direction of the debate if they can just frame it correctly. Just like a suspected criminal wearing a suit to court, activists are aware that form can be as important as content. In this particular debate, where death itself is regarded as a dirty word, the language in which they present their arguments is an influential and emotive agent provocateur. So they have been working hard, at their conferences and in smaller forums, to find a universally acceptable linguistic form in which to express their goals.

The slogan "right to die," for example, is criticized by all sides involved for being a meaningless term: Death is an inevitable "right" for us all, and critics say that the phrase does nothing to define the real issue at stake. For the same reasons, activists hate the epithet "death with dignity"—a meaningless bromide that they fear puts an unrealistic pressure on a dying patient.

"Death is real and messy," says James Goodwin, M.D., head of the Center on Aging at the University of Texas in Galveston. "Very few people die 'good' deaths, deaths with real dignity. But that should never become a judgment. We can't demand a certain style of dying." Ira Byock, president of the

Academy of Hospice and Palliative Medicine in Missoula, Montana, agrees. "There's an inherent dignity in the human condition that never changes," he says. "People don't become 'undignified' just because they become physically dependent. I won't accept that my patients are undignified in their dying."

Then there's that ubiquitous phrase "physician-assisted suicide," which proponents of the practice particularly dislike: It's an inauspicious term for what they wish to express. Advocates explain that "suicide," with its stirring, even sinful, overtones, falsely suggests that someone is prematurely ending his life, whereas the truth is that a terminally ill person—someone who is already dying—is choosing to end his misery a little sooner by hastening his inevitable demise.

Opponents of the practice dislike the word "suicide" for other reasons. Ljubisa Dragovic, the Oakland County chief medical examiner, says that in his view, calling the act "suicide" shifts the responsibility from the physician to the patient. "It's nonsense to call it suicide because the patient needs the help of the physician to do it," he says. "Let's call it what it is—voluntary euthanasia."

If saying "death" instead of "suicide" automatically lowers the emotional climate, as advocates suggest, then how about "self-deliverance," with its misty connotations of some heroic and gentle end? Is that so euphemistic as to be meaningless? And does "euthanasia"—even if it's voluntary—sound too frightening, too involuntary, to be acceptable?

The consensus among supporters is that using the phrase "physician-hastened death" is better than "physician-assisted death," although it would be better still to eliminate the word "physician" entirely. "We need to make it clear that this is the choice of the *patient,*" explains a physician. "Maybe 'medically hastened death' does it best."

When Derek Humphry founded ERGO! in 1993, one of his first tasks was to commission a poll to assess the impact of the "right to die" terminology on the general public. (Humphry himself says he has always favored the phrase "right to choose to die.")

The survey staff asked 1000 people whether they would vote for a law spelled out in blunt language, and then asked a different 1000 people if they would vote for a law couched in euphemisms. What they found was that people, especially women, tended to prefer euphemisms.

For example, while 55 percent of people would vote for a law allowing the terminally ill to choose "euthanasia," 65 percent supported the right of the terminally ill to choose "death with dignity" over prolonging life. While 44 percent would allow "physician-assisted suicide," 51 percent felt greater sympathy for "physician aid in dying." And while 44 percent would allow a terminally ill person to choose a "lethal injection," 50 percent would approve a "medical procedure."

Humphry says he was not surprised by the findings. But he thinks they do not mean that dealing with death issues euphemistically is necessarily the best way to proceed.

"What we all have to decide is whether it is good for society to continue the slide into greater reliance on euphemistic words and phrases," he says. "By using Orwellian 'doublespeak' we might be letting ourselves in for procedures and conclusions which we do not fully comprehend at the time of decision making. On the other hand, perhaps euphemisms allow people to come to grips with brutal facts which, stated another way, would be repugnant to them."

Perhaps the best example of this new move toward euphemistic words is the general acceptance given to the term "exit bag," the more-or-less neutral words used to describe a bag that is placed over a person's head to ensure death. In 1998, the American Dialect Society, which every year awards prizes for words and terms recently introduced into the English language, gave "exit bag" their first prize for "most euphemistic word." Obviously, the society felt that the term effectively removed from the language the aura of repugnance and unacceptability that many people, even supporters of assisted dying, say they feel in connection with this particular practice.

It is surely not surprising that Dr. Kevorkian, operating, as it were, in his own universe, has fashioned his personal lexicon of death. He too dislikes the term "euthanasia," he says, but his objection is that it implies that assisting a death can be practiced by anyone. When a physician takes part, the deed is "medicide," and when a physician like himself is a committed practitioner of "medicide," he becomes an "obitiatrist," devoted to the specialty of "obitiatry." What's more, Kevorkian's goal is to set up special clinics—"obitoriums"— where people can come for humane, assisted death.

"Medicide is euthanasia, but euthanasia may not be medicide," Kevorkian explains in his book *Prescription: Medicide.* "And obitiatry is medicide, but medicide may not be obitiatry.

"The time has come to let medicide extend a comforting hand to those slipping into the valley of death, and to let obitiatry extract from their ebbing vitality the power to illuminate some of its darkest recesses for those who come after them."

Does that clarify the goals? Or do the semantics of the "medically hastened self-deliverance with dignity" movement still need some work?

Many right-to-die activists, befuddled by semantics, have found a more direct way of communicating: via new technology. It's their sophisticated understanding of the technology's potential to further their goals that places this particular cause at the brink of a new millenium. Unlike the "underground" crusades of the past, where messages were whispered furtively along a meandering grapevine of sympathizers, the contemporary right-to-die movement can disseminate its information simply, cheaply, and instantly, privately or publicly, anywhere in the world via the Internet. A movement that spreads word of its activities chiefly by means of cyberspace, that uses computers to select patients for death, and that has even devised ways of enabling the machines to actually bring about death (as Australia's Dr. Nitschke did to perform the world's first three fully legal, medically assisted suicides) is truly a movement in concert with its times.

For most dedicated members, the "must read" component of the computer's offerings is the ERGO! electronic mailing list. It has more than 600 regular subscribers whose correspondence ranges from noting international RTD developments or commenting on the latest legal moves to posting pleas for effective methods of "self-deliverance."

"Dear good people," read one recent e-mail. "Where can we get carbon monoxide to breathe to death? No one seems to have an answer. Strange. Where di [sic] Dr K get it? Easy, painless, just breat [sic] in and die. Right? Thank you."

With as many as a dozen messages transmitted every day, the mailing list can be a lively platform, subject to the same irritations in the name of "democratic freedom" as any other public forum. It has been infiltrated and frequently "flamed" by angry opposition groups who, in dramatic tones, accuse the list's supporters of harboring a secret agenda for plotting death for the weak and disabled. Because of these persistent accusations, some frustrated regulars have "unsubscribed" from the list, including its most prolific contributor, Canadian activist John Hofsess. When Hofsess declared that his disgust with right-to-life infiltration of the list had driven him away, dozens of messages appeared imploring him to stay. But Hofsess remained firm. "This is no longer a right-to-die mailing list," he wrote angrily. "It has increasingly become a service for prolife 'lurkers' who parasitically exploit my contributions and those of others. . . . I will not participate in any forum which welcomes thugs like these. If [it] evolves into something higher, I may return." Humphry, in an attempt to "clean up" his list, changed it from unmoderated to moderated. And after an absence of several months, Hofsess started his own private mailing list, Nothing But The News, which provides for its handpicked members a significant service by posting news reports and summaries of developments around the world.

Hofsess's electronic contributions to the cause have been prodigious. Along with Humphry, he initiated DeathTalk, "the world's first on-line chat area specializing in 'right-to-die' issues and problems," and DeathNET, a site on the World Wide Web that he still runs in a loose partnership with Humphry. DeathNET is a skillfully designed electronic library, offering easy access to news, history, and anticipated developments, as well as to relevant literature and death-related products. DeathNET has logged visits from activists and academics around the world, and from students doing research on end-of-life concerns. Hofsess welcomes these browsers especially, as he is hopeful that the next generation will have a greater understanding of right-to-die issues than the older one does.

Today, almost all of the different right-to-die organizations have their own websites, as do most major legal, bioethical, and medical institutions. Through the efforts of Janet Good, the Internet has also become a way for would-be patients to contact Dr. Kevorkian. When 63-year-old Shirley Kline flew from California to Michigan to become the 32nd patient to receive the doctor's help in dying, the entire operation had been arranged via the Internet by Good and Kline's closest friend. Good has corresponded with several of Dr Kevorkian's patients this way. She became so close to Austin Bastable, a dying Canadian activist, through their computerized communications that Bastable came to her home when he decided he was ready to receive Kevorkian's services. (Bastable also left a "Last Hurrah"—a farewell message on his homepage. "It will be a black mark on Canadian history, in years to come, that people like Sue Rodriguez [another Canadian who fought to receive physician-assisted death] and myself had to struggle so enormously simply to be allowed to be in charge of our own health-care decisions," Bastable wrote. "We are victims of an antiquated and irrational law.")

Bastable's survivors are as determined as he was to change that outmoded law. No matter what the Supreme Court would rule, advocates pledged at the Hemlock conference, they would continue to fight, state by state. As the meeting wound down, its delegates, focusing outwards once more, split into two distinct groups. One group lingered in the meeting rooms, reluctant to leave, intent on electing new board members and discussing the tasks that lay immediately ahead. The other group, evidently sated with 3 days of death talk, piled onto a tour bus and headed downtown, suddenly keen to feel the mountain air in their nostrils, and to talk of life in a candlelit restaurant.

This group, at a glance, consisted mainly of the movement's rank and file, for whom this conference had been as much a social event as a political one. They had learned what they wanted to find out—how many Seconal to hoard, how most effectively to approach their state representative about changing the law—and now they were ready to return to their everyday lives.

On the ride back to the airport, I sat beside a middle-aged woman to whom I had been introduced at the conference. She was a jolly woman, a semiprofessional entertainer and longtime Hemlock Society member who had come to Denver from Hawaii, and said she still had a few days to go before she returned. In fact, she admitted, she was on her way to another conference, this one in Las Vegas, this one about clowning. From death in Denver to clowning in Vegas. Truly, from the sublime to the ridiculous.

♦ CHAPTER 9 ♦

The Medical
Establishment
A Fortress Divided

I am dying with the help of too many physicians.
—Alexander the Great

Within the right-to-die community, physicians have come to
be regarded as "enemies of the people."

Geoffrey Fieger, Jack Kevorkian's lawyer, calls them "intellectual hypocrites," retired Washington physician Hugh
Lawrence, M.D., says they're "gutless wonders," and Richard
MacDonald, M.D., medical director of the Hemlock Society,
concedes that physician-assisted death "is a challenge to the
medical community that we have met very poorly."

Unfortunately for the activists, physicians are the most
crucial players in the right-to-die debate, after the patients
themselves. If changes are to be made in the law, it will be
physicians—not relatives or loved ones—who will help patients achieve the deaths they seek. This fact has thrown the

profession into a profound crisis of conscience, creating a climate of mistrust and fear, and dividing medical institutions and professional bodies. It has even opened a rift between a new generation of physicians, who tend to be more sympathetic to the idea, and their older colleagues, who, on the whole, remain vehemently opposed. (In preparation for the Supreme Court hearing on the issue, the 40,000 member American Medical Association submitted an "amicus" brief to the Court, recommending rejection of assisted dying. The American Medical Students Association, which represents 30,000 physicians in training nationwide and calls itself "the future of medicine in the United States," submitted a brief in support.)

At the heart of the issue is a fundamental philosophical tenet of medicine: Should the physician's role be strictly to aid and comfort? Or should it be to end suffering as well— even in cases where ending suffering means ending life?

Opponents of assisted dying say physicians need look no further than the Hippocratic oath, which puts it quite simply: "I will give no deadly medicine to anyone if asked, nor suggest any such counsel."

"Assisting a patient to die is fundamentally in opposition to a physician's ethical code, and we would be concerned that it would affect the trusting relationship that exists between physician and patient," says Thomas Reardon, M.D., vice chairman of the American Medical Association's Board of Trustees.

With proper pain control and end-of-life care, physicians say, no patient should ever want to hasten his death. "Pain is one of the compelling factors that lead patients to request physician-assisted suicide and euthanasia," says Kathleen M. Foley, M.D., chief of the pain service at Memorial Sloan-Kettering Cancer Center in New York. The problem is, as Foley admits, that today's physicians still tend to undermedicate patients for their pain. They either refuse to administer large enough doses of painkilling drugs like morphine for fear of turning a patient into an addict, or they are ignorant of sophisticated advances in treatment such as nerve blocks, which can bring comfort to all but the most severely suffering.

To compound the problems, studies show that most physicians are undertrained to deal with the specific issues and problems of dying. Foley points to a survey of 1168 accredited residency programs around the country that practice family, internal, pediatric, and geriatric medicine. The survey reveals that almost 15 percent of these programs offered no formal training in terminal care, and that most of the students attending them coordinated the care of just ten or fewer dying patients a year. The signs for the future don't look much better: A 1993 study of medical schools published in the *American Journal of Public Health* found that methods of teaching about death and dying needed to be radically overhauled in order to update a new generation of physicians on state-of-the-art treatment and care for terminal patients. If these issues are properly addressed, Foley believes, the call for assisted death would virtually disappear.

Yet no one in today's beleaguered health care system expects to see improvements anytime soon. And in the meantime, they say, when patients are dying, despite all of the painkillers in the world, what they need most is to feel that their physicians won't abandon them.

"With a terminal illness, a physician's role is to ease a number of transitions for the patient—first to help him to live better for as long as he can, and when that becomes impossible, to help him in his transition towards death," says internist Howard Grossman, assistant clinical professor of medicine at St. Lukes-Roosevelt Hospital, Columbia University.

Advocates of assisted dying agree. They point to the popularity of Kevorkian's actions as proof of people's desire to have their physicians help them die. Although many of Kevorkian's patients have in fact been physically able to perform a suicidal act themselves, they don't want to—they want to die painlessly, with the help, and in the presence, of a professional. And the fact that Kevorkian's services are still so much in demand shows that, while it remains illegal, only a very few professionals are prepared to be there for their patients, to help them die.

Seventy-year-old general practitioner Andrew Porter is one of the few physicians who is. Porter has been helping his patients to die for more than 30 years. He considers it an integral part of his work as a family physician and a healer—a modern-day "shaman," as he calls himself. When I met him in his simple, cosy office, he was pleased to see me. He said it felt auspicious, and he thought it was finally time to step out of the shadows and talk about what he does. For a while, Porter considered discussing the issue under his real name, but given the criminal nature of his deeds, and given all that he still plans to do in his professional life, he eventually decided to conceal his identity under the pseudonym of Andrew Porter.

"I believe the way I practice medicine—the whole picture—is exactly the way it should be practiced, although it has been scary and lonely over the years," he says. "I've been in uncharted territory in the realms of American medicine. But I'm increasingly sure I've been doing it the right way."

It was during his training at Harvard Medical School, in the early 1950s, that Porter discovered the kind of physician he wanted to be: not a specialist or a surgeon but an old-fashioned family physician, someone who makes house calls and knows all of the family members, someone whom the patient will call for any crisis in his life, and who "will hang off the bathroom ceiling by his toes, if that's what it takes to heal them," he says.

Porter and his first wife, Lily, started a family practice back in the 1960s as a "mom-and-pop store" in an elegant neighborhood on Chicago's North Shore. Colleagues and friends warned them that such an outdated enterprise was unlikely to take off, but the Porters quickly made it thrive. It's easy to see why. Contact, warm and human, is what Porter is all about; he's a hugger and a toucher, humane and direct, emanating the kind of reassuring authority that one would hope for in one's family physician. He's also endlessly curious, interested in the people he meets—in their childhoods, their beliefs, their passions—because he believes that the relationship he forms with his patients is all important in helping them live a long and healthy life.

"Trust is the key, "he says. "If you trust your physician, you can live longer and better." (It's because of the lack of choice involved in finding a physician that Porter is so opposed to managed care.)

But, no matter how long and well one lives, at the end of life always comes death. It is, as Porter believes, "the moment of truth, the most important stage of life." For him, it's a stage that should hold no fear—as long as it's approached in the right way. Porter firmly believes that there's a right way and a wrong way to die. The wrong way to die is with unresolved stresses and issues left hanging between oneself and one's family and friends. The right way is to work it all out, which, according to Porter, frees the body to take its own peaceful journey. That is why, he explains, he will assist his patients to die—but only if he feels they have done what they can, and with the cooperation of their loved ones, to prepare their way toward death. "I consciously try to do what I feel is the job of a physician," he says.

Porter remembers well the first death he assisted, some 30 years ago. His patient was a man in his late 60s who had for years struggled valiantly with thyroid cancer. For a long time, the disease was held at bay, but suddenly it returned with a vengeance, and spread quickly through his chest cavity. The man became breathless and afraid that he would eventually suffocate. He asked Porter to help him end his life.

"I told him, 'It's not my job to give you the weapon of your death and just stand by and watch you kill yourself," Porter says. "I explained, 'My job is to help you deal with the most important crisis of your, and your family's, life.' Then I said that before I could do anything, I would have to meet with his whole family, and I did. The first time we all met, his wife was totally against him killing himself, and his three sons—well, they were just listening at that stage. I made a series of home visits to the family and showed them, in fits and starts, that there was a lot of anger among them that needed to be dealt with. For a start, the man was furious: He was furious that the disease was getting out of control, and he wanted to kill himself as a kind of punishment to God. I said that wouldn't do any good, and I tried to show him that his thinking about it was all wrong. I convinced him to do it with the cooperation of his family, not to spite them or himself."

For a long while, Porter heard nothing from his patient. Finally, almost 4 months later, the man telephoned and asked Porter to come by. When he did, he found the family all in agreement about the man's impending act. They had worked out many of their tensions, and the wife was finally ready to let her husband go. They asked Porter to be present at his patient's death, but once again, the physician had to refuse.

"I realized that it wouldn't be right," he says. "I had to show the family that they were on their own with this act, and that, if it were done right, no one would be hurt by it, that they would all find peace."

The family understood. So when the time came for the man to take his deadly draft, they sat at his bedside with him, as he slipped peacefully from sleep to unconsciousness to death.

In the eyes of many Americans, these actions make Andrew Porter something of a hero, one of a rare breed of physicians who is prepared to perform his duties to their logical, inevitable conclusion. But in the eyes of the law and the many physicians and private citizens who support it, Porter is a criminal who has violated the integrity of his profession.

"Our fear is that physicians who perform assisted suicide are on a very slippery slope," says the AMA's Thomas Reardon. "The first couple of times they are asked to write prescriptions for lethal drugs will be very difficult, and then the next few times will be a little less so. By the tenth time, it'll be no big deal—just as if they're writing a prescription for penicillin."

Other opponents fear that the categories of patients being given help will start to expand from the terminally ill to the chronically ill and eventually to those who have simply grown tired of life. And then maybe even to those who do not want to die, but whom society considers an unnecessary load: the disabled, the elderly, those whose families make them feel they are a burden, those who no longer know what is going on.

The potential for abuse first became the subject of public debate as a result of an article published in 1988 in the *Journal of the American Medical Association,* entitled "It's Over, Debbie." The anonymous physician who wrote the article identified himself only as a gynecology resident in a large private hospital. He wrote how he was on duty late one night when he was called to assist a 20-year-old woman, evidently in the final, agonizing stages of ovarian cancer. As he came to her bedside, he wrote, her only words were "Let's get this over with." In response, the physician injected her with 20 milligrams of morphine sulfate and watched as within seconds, her breathing slowed to a normal rate and she managed to fall asleep.

"I waited for the inevitable next effect [of the morphine] of depressing the respiratory drive," the anonymous physician wrote. "With clocklike certainty, within four minutes the breathing rate slowed even more, then became irregular, then ceased. . . . It's over, Debbie."

This physician's admission caused a torrent of outrage—not just within the medical profession, but among law enforcers as well. The public prosecutor went to great lengths to discover the author's identity, and made it clear that if he had been able to do so (which he wasn't), he would have prosecuted him for homicide. Physicians also went out of their way to assure the public that the unknown physician had acted counter to everything physicians stand for: that assisting death, in general, is a crime in most states in the country. Assisting death without even having been requested to do so is a crime of the most serious kind: murder.

The issue of the patient's request is central to the debate about physician aid in dying. First of all, it defines who may qualify for such aid, and automatically rules out comatose patients like Nancy Cruzan and Karen Ann Quinlan who could not make their own requests known, and whose fates were thus left for the courts to decide. Although the Quinlan case established the precedent for physicians being able to withdraw life-sustaining measures from patients, none of the changes currently being proposed in the law would affect the future for patients in comas or persistent vegetative states, and no one is proposing that they should. Advocates stress that their goal is to legalize assisted death only in cases where patients are able to ask for it specifically and repeatedly.

In fact, physicians who support assisted death are quick to point out how cautious they would be in such cases. Not only should the patient be competent and able to request help, they say, but there should be other safeguards in place to ensure that the measure only rarely qualifies as an appropriate act—and is only rarely used. So they also insist that patients who want their help must be terminally, rather than chronically, ill. (By terminally ill, the medical establishment means that someone has an estimated 6 months or less to live.) This distinction would rule out most of the people who have sought Kevorkian's aid in dying; people who, although suffering, could have continued to live for years with their condition, people with Alzheimer's disease, for example, or multiple sclerosis. What's more, under the proposed new laws, physicians would be able to administer only to those who can orchestrate their deaths themselves: In short, they say, they are not advocating voluntary euthanasia, let alone involuntary euthanasia, but a form of facilitating death that puts the patient fully in control of the action.

Just as activists are anxious to get their "hastened death" terminology right, so the medical profession is concerned to explain the technical distinctions between "physician aid in dying" and "euthanasia"—active and passive, voluntary and involuntary. Advocates say that clarifying these terms is vital to explain physicians' different degrees of participation in each act, as well as the different degrees of illegality between them.

For example, while voluntary euthanasia is illegal throughout the United States, there are still a half-dozen states that have no laws governing physician aid in dying, and no effective policy for treating violators. (Michigan is the prime example of this, and many believe that the main reason Kevorkian has managed to escape punishment so far is because of the state's muddled legislation that has had prosecutors resorting to archaic English common law in their efforts to convict him.) In fact, no physician in the country has yet been made to serve a prison term for compassionately helping a dying person to end her life. But there are serious repercussions to the act other than jail: Dr. Timothy Quill, the New York physician who has admitted helping his patient, "Diane," to die, points out that "the risk of an expensive, publicized professional and legal inquiry will be prohibitive for most physicians, and will certainly keep the practice covert and isolating for those who participate."

Physician aid in dying is different from voluntary euthanasia in one important way: Even though the patient may get a physician's help, such as a prescription for a lethal dose of drugs, it is up to the patient whether or not he administers it. Preferably, he will do so when the physician is not even present, thereby emphasizing that the impetus is purely his own. With active euthanasia, on the other hand, even when the act is voluntary, the physician not only makes the means of death available, but is also the person who administers it. Having the physician, not the patient, do the deed automatically increases the potential for abuse or error. With involuntary euthanasia, which takes place without the patient's request and perhaps even consciousness, the chances of abuse are high: Involuntary euthanasia, in most people's eyes, is tantamount to murder.

"The difference has to do with what the physician does," said Marcia Angell, executive editor of the *New England Journal of Medicine,* when she debated the issue at a seminar hosted by the Death with Dignity Education Center. "When the physician is considered passive, that's supposed to be good, and when the physician is active, it's considered bad."

According to Angell, withholding or withdrawing life-sustaining treatment, which became legal as a result of the Quinlan case, is considered passive. If a patient dies as a result of a respirator being removed or an antibiotic being withheld, the cause of death is attributed to the underlying illness, not the withholding of treatment. Euthanasia—injecting a lethal drug—on the other hand, is active, because it is the action taken that has caused the patient's death. Physician-assisted suicide—writing a prescription for fatal drugs—is considered an intermediate between the two, as the physician does not actually administer the drugs, and the patient's action is therefore morally more ambiguous.

Some argue that these distinctions are spurious: Many physicians say that often, an act of omission is the same as an act of commission, especially when the motive and the result are the same. In addition, depriving an individual of food or oxygen can be a much more protracted and less merciful act than giving them a fast-acting lethal dose of medicine.

"There's nothing passive about pulling a respirator tube out of a patient's throat," says internist Grossman. "It's far less active simply to write a prescription."

To make matters more complicated, another way of making the definitions is from the patients' point of view. Lawyers, such as the Ninth and Second Circuit judges who decided the 1996 California and New York cases in favor of physician assistance of dying patients, have argued that the physician's role is irrelevant: that what is important is the active or passive role the patient takes. In this case, assisted suicide is "good" because it requires the active participation of the patient, who by definition must take a deliberate action such as swallowing pills. Voluntary euthanasia (for example, a lethal injection) and involuntary euthanasia can both be carried out with the patient being quite passive— sometimes even unaware—which the judges consider "bad," as they did with "Debbie."

* * *

The "Debbie" article shed light on one of the medical profession's most controversial secrets: the use of morphine. It's common for physicians to give morphine as a way of alleviating pain and suffering. But morphine has a "double effect," as it is frequently called, and as all physicians know: It depresses breathing and ends life. Many physicians prescribe it for this very reason. The "double effect" even has the endorsement of the Catholic Church, so long as the drugs are ostensibly given to bring about relief of suffering, and not death, even if death is then inevitable. As the church put it in a 1975 directive from the National Conference of Catholic Bishops, "it is not euthanasia to give a dying person sedatives and analgesics for the alleviation of pain, even though they may deprive the patient of the use of reason, or shorten his life."

Physicians know that certain drugs *do* shorten patients' lives, and they often prescribe them precisely for that reason. It's a form of assisted dying that has been practiced, with full awareness, for decades. And yet, acknowledging its use as such remains a taboo.

"This is the dirty little secret of medicine," Grossman says. "This is the tremendous burden that physicians have carried with them for a long, long time, the fact that they already help people out. It's time that it was brought out into the open and talked about."

There are no figures to indicate exactly how common physician-assisted death is in the United States, but it's thought that the practice is and has been widespread for hundreds of years. In 1992, an informal survey by the American Society of Internal Medicine showed that out of 402 physicians polled, almost a quarter had been asked for help in dying by a terminally ill patient, and of those asked, 40 percent had agreed. Given the illegal nature of assisting death, it is hard to know how representative these figures really are. But experts believe they are probably a fair estimate.

Because the practice is known to go on, some argue that the law should be left as it is: "Hey, if it's already available, then let it stay that way," the argument goes. "People already get what they want." Untrue, insist those on the other side. Secrecy not only places an unfair burden on physicians who must make those fateful decisions alone and cannot consult their peers; it also places an unfair amount of power in the physicians' hands. "What this hypocritical, paternalistic system does is to encourage disrespect for the law and encourage physicians to assume they're above the law—that the law applies to others and not to them," says Charles Baron, professor of law at Boston College Law School. Keeping assisted suicide illegal, Baron says, leads to "rank injustice. It undermines the rule of law and the principles of open government. The system doesn't protect against abuse, it protects us from knowing how much abuse is going on out there. It's not protecting patients."

But physicians who reject assisting patients in dying argue that it's not a question of power, but of ethical beliefs. The rift within the medical profession is between those who believe that it is right—even a duty—to help a suffering patient to die, and those who feel that providing such help is not merely a crime but a travesty of medicine. According to the American Medical Association, which has officially opposed physician-assisted suicide on numerous occasions since the late 1930s, "The power to assist in intentionally taking the life of a patient is antithetical to the central mission of healing that guides both medicine and nursing. It is a power that most physicians and nurses do not want and could not control."

So firmly entrenched is the belief in healing that many health professionals see death as failure. That is why, perhaps, so many of them have such a hard time confronting death with their patients. A startling study published early in 1996 discovered that, despite 20 years of living wills and "do not resuscitate" orders, most physicians are still ignoring them, and forcibly give their patients lifesaving measures they do not want. The SUPPORT study, as it is known, was funded by the Robert Wood Johnson Foundation and conducted over a 10-year period in major medical facilities nationwide. It showed that even when patients had completed advance medical directives and DNR forms, when it came to treatment, their directives were either "misplaced" or simply overridden. According to the study, 50 percent of dying patients suffered severe pain in the last 3 days of their lives; at least 38 percent spent 10 days or more in intensive care, either on life-support systems or comatose. And 31 percent of patients' families used up their life savings on paying for futile end-of-life medical care.

The New York advocacy group Choice in Dying maintains that many patients' wishes—especially their wishes not to be given invasive treatment—are ignored because there are many advantages for the physician who continues to treat. First, health care providers are actually rewarded for the treatments they provide—no matter whether those treatments have been requested or rejected. Second, state laws on advance directives operate in such a way that there are no real risks involved in ignoring a patient's specific requests. Although 48 states are legally bound to recognize the validity of living wills, in reality 46 of them permit physicians to refuse to comply with them if they find a patient's requests either morally, religiously, or professionally unacceptable.

"Unfortunately, the absence of penalty provisions in most advance directive laws fosters a belief among health care providers that noncompliance is legally acceptable," argues Choice in Dying. The organization believes that the only way to remedy this state of affairs is to impose penalties: if they provide unwanted services, the organization suggests, physicians should be made to pay for them.

And patients are beginning to resist, bringing accusations of battery on physicians who foist unwanted treatment on them. The precedents for this go back to the Cruzan case in 1990, when the Supreme Court noted that in common law, "Even the touching of one person by another without consent and without legal justification is a battery."

The legal repercussions of a battery conviction can be catastrophic, as a Michigan hospital, Genesys St. Joseph, discovered in 1996 when a jury awarded $16 million to the family of Brenda Young, a 38-year-old woman severely brain damaged by a series of seizures. The case is on appeal, and the judge has indicated that he intends to reduce the award, but nonetheless the family is certain to walk away with a substantial sum.

In 1977, Young was a healthy 19-year-old when she suffered a brain hemorrhage. Physicians discovered she had abnormal blood vessels in her brain and warned her that her condition would certainly get worse. In anticipation, Young appointed her mother, Ramona Osgood, to be her health advocate with durable powers of attorney so she would be able to make her daughter's health care wishes clear. Young's wishes were that, if she became incompetent, she would want neither resuscitation nor ventilation nor food and water. But in 1992, after suffering a massive seizure, she was taken to Genesys St. Joseph, where the medical staff chose to override her wishes. They put her on a ventilator, tube fed her, maintained her through a 2-month coma, and then, having weaned her off the respirator, discharged her back to her mother's tiny bungalow in a state of severe and permanent brain damage. Over the next 4 years, repeated brain seizures left Young totally dependent on care and in need of restraining in her bed, where she would flail around and scream at blood-curdling volume, sometimes for as long as 20 hours a day. Because of her screaming, her mother could not find a nursing home that would admit her, and she was not able to afford the around-the-clock care her daughter needed. Currently, Medicaid provides her with 11 hours of daily care during the week, and 5 hours on weekends. The rest of the time, Osgood, almost 70 years old and herself ailing, must care for her afflicted daughter on her own. "She has been worn down to a frazzle by it all," says the family's attorney, Clark Shanahan. "When Brenda is conscious, she indicates that she wants to die: She draws her one unparalyzed arm across her throat, or she gets out the words, "Kill Me," but all this family wants is the right to refuse treatment. They are not even asking for someone to help her die. To me, this case shows the enormous indifference of institutional medicine, the arrogance of their attitude that "we know best.'"

Young's case is just one of a new wave of lawsuits aimed at hospitals, nursing homes, and individual health care workers. "The public's patience is frayed," says a member of Choice in Dying. "Unfortunately, in the present climate, many patients and families believe that they automatically lose control when they enter a hospital. Too often, they believe that the only way to be heard is to establish an antagonistic relationship with their health care providers."

For the lucky ones, this need not be so, as those who have close, cooperative relationships with their physicians are much more likely to feel in control—and to get their physicians to agree to help them die.

Timothy Quill made his historic decision to help his patient "Diane" to die based on the longstanding association between them. He had already known Diane for many years when he diagnosed her with leukemia, and he was familiar with her medical history, her family, and her particular tolerance for pain and suffering. She had already had to deal with alcoholism, depression, and a bout with vaginal cancer. Now, she was confronted with the prospect of toxic chemotherapy and bone marrow transplantation, with only a slim chance of surviving the treatment, let alone the disease. When Diane decided not to subject herself to any more medical intervention, but to live out the remaining weeks of her life with her family, Quill supported her decision. And when she asked him for a lethal dose of drugs to help her die before she lost control, Quill agonized about what to do and eventually decided to help her.

"I wrote the prescription with an uneasy feeling about the boundaries I was exploring—spiritual, legal, professional and personal," he wrote. "Yet I also felt strongly that I was setting her free to get the most out of the time she had left, and to maintain dignity and control on her own terms until her death."

It was one particular aspect of Diane's death that prompted Quill to go public with his confession and that disturbs him to this day: Out of fear of incriminating her family in her dying, Diane made them leave her when she took her lethal dose, and she died alone while they were out.

"I wonder whether the image of Diane's final aloneness will persist in the minds of her family, or if they will remember more the intense, meaningful months they had together before she died," he concluded. "I wonder why Diane, who gave so much to so many of us, had to be alone for the last hour of her life."

When published, Quill's confession had a powerful effect on his peers. It was as if he had opened an artery: Admissions of complicity came pouring out. Quill received some 2000 letters, mainly from physicians around the country who, like himself, had helped a patient to die—some just once, some repeatedly—and who had kept their guilty secret for years, often decades.

Quill says that when he published his article, he had no thoughts about where it would lead him. He says he wasn't planning to become a leader for the cause of physician-assisted death, although that is surely what he has become. He was the main plaintiff in the 1994 lawsuit *Vacco v. Quill,* which asked the courts to strike down the New York law prohibiting physician-assisted death for terminally ill patients, and which ended up before the Supreme Court in 1997. He spends an increasing amount of his time writing and lecturing on his subject at professional meetings and ethics committees, to medical students, on grand rounds, and before right-to-die groups. He tries to keep his advocacy work down to no more than two or three times a month. At the same time, he remains a busy family physician, as well as associate chief of medicine at the Genesee Hospital in Rochester.

The earnest, soft-spoken Quill, with his owlish, bespectacled face, balding hair, and close-cropped beard, does not display the passion or natural charisma that one would expect from such an engaged campaigner. But, maybe for that very reason, he has become a much-favored spokesman for his cause—a deliberately "moderate" presence among the emotional hotheads steaming off around him. It is an image he tries to exploit; describing himself as "someone trying to articulate the middle ground between the forces pushing this issue to the brink," Quill decries the "radicals" of the movement, such as Kevorkian and Humphry, for their extremism, and allies himself with "responsible" organizations such as the Death with Dignity Education Center, whose self-described mission is to promote "a comprehensive, humane, responsive system of care for terminally-ill patients." Quill says he shares their belief that "aid in dying should be a last resort, rather than a rights issue."

One of Quill's contributions to the movement has been to draw up, with colleagues, a list of safeguards for physicians to follow if assisted death were to be legalized. The safeguards, published in the *New England Journal of Medicine* and adopted by the DDEC as their official guidelines, are deliberately conservative—conservative enough to make the NEJM's Angell wonder whether too many safeguards would act as a deterrent, even to eligible patients.

But Quill stands firm. "If we end up with the nth degree of euthanasia on demand, that's a very bad outcome," he says. "It's only worthwhile if it allows people to respond to extreme suffering."

Quill's critics—and he has plenty—say that his moderate image is a sham. In a scathing article in the *Village Voice* that describes Quill as euthanasia's "poster boy," writer Nat

Hentoff quotes remarks by Quill that indicate that his criteria for selecting patients for help in dying are in reality far wider than he pretends. Hentoff claims that Quill has talked about stretching eligibility from patients with terminal illness to those with "an intolerable quality of life" and even to include those facing the vague prospect of "dying in an undignified, unaesthetic, absurd and existentially unacceptable condition."

When challenged on these views before a congressional hearing, Hentoff reports, Quill said he had only been exploring such possibilities "on an intellectual level." He still believed in restricting the practice "as a last resort for the terminally ill."

"You have gone back to [that] position then?," a congressman asked. To which Quill replied, "I think for the current situation, yes."

It is curious that, despite their reverence for the notion of healing, many physicians express the fear that legalizing physician-assisted death could lead to a "slippery slope." It is as if they are afraid that, given license, they would find out how murderous they really are, and begin "knocking off" their patients with nonchalance. "We are simply afraid that we'll prove to be human," one physician explained to me. "We'll make mistakes, errors of judgment, bad calls—and they'll be irrevocable."

"Physicians make life-and-death decisions every day," replies Dr. Angell, who says that what's really at stake is patients' basic trust in their physicians' decision-making abilities. "No endeavor can be made immune to all abuse, and if assisted suicide is made legal, there will be problematic cases," she says. "The question is, whether the difficult cases will be outweighed by the benefits that terminally suffering patients will get."

Over the years, Andrew Porter's experiences have shown him that both of these reactions are valid. While he is a committed believer in his right to help his patients to die—and their right to ask him—he also can't dismiss the dangers of the slippery slope, for he has been down it himself, with terrible consequences. That single foray into forbidden territory, he says, has left him with little doubt of its wrongfulness—not from a criminal point of view, but from a moral one.

When Porter agreed to meet me that morning at his local coffeeshop, I'm not sure if he was already planning to reveal what he did. But suddenly, he came to a part of his story that I could see he was reluctant to delve into. I could feel him deciding whether to step back or take the plunge. He pushed away his almost untouched plate of eggs, put his elbows on the table in front of him, and rubbed his elegant hands over his face. I tried to jog him just a little, then waited. Finally, he steeled himself and began to recount how he learned—the hard way—about the limits to a physician's powers, and the territory that lies beyond his domain.

"It was the only time in my life that I agreed to administer a lethal injection," Porter says finally with a deep, pained sigh. "It was a terrifying experience—one of the worst moments in my life."

Against his better judgment, he says, he agreed to "kill" the mother of his best friend, Peter. "He and his wife, Caroline, were the closest people in my life. I couldn't say no," he relates.

"I had known Peter's mother, Victoria, since I was a very young man, and I revered her," he goes on. "She was a marvelous woman, a social worker and a writer, and we would see each other regularly at family gatherings, a couple of times a year. But as she grew into her 90s, she went blind, almost deaf, and she could hardly walk. She went into an old age complex and decided she didn't want to go on. She asked her son—well, she commanded him—to kill her. But he couldn't, of course, and so he asked me if I would. I couldn't turn him down, although I should have—I should never have agreed to kill her."

Porter said the enterprise was marred from the start. "Firstly, I didn't have the guts to confront Victoria directly, so I never spoke to her beforehand about what I was going to do," he says. "And I should have known that no physician should ever take care of their loved ones. It was all so wrong."

The nightmarish sequence of events that followed haunts Porter still. "I traveled to Indiana, to Victoria's home, where the three of us, Peter, Caroline, and I, sat at her bedside and I explained what I was going to do. She understood, and agreed. Then I hypnotized her to calm her down, and put her to sleep. Just before I was to do it, I asked Peter to go into the other room. Then, as I was putting the solution I was going to use into the syringe, Victoria began to stir. As I watched her, her movements got stronger and stronger so that she started thrashing around, and then went almost into convulsions. I felt as though a devil had been let loose, as if she was trying to get at me for what I was doing. Caroline had to lay on top of her, and hold her head, so I could inject the morphine into her. Eventually, I injected enough into her so that she finally quieted and died."

But the tribulations weren't over. Porter had told his friend that he needed a guarantee that there would be no difficulty with the signing of the death certificate. Peter would need to find a physician who knew ahead of time what was happening, and who would be willing to sign the death certificate with no questions asked. As it turned out, the physician was off duty that day and in the middle of that night, Peter received a call from the funeral parlor saying that the death certificate hadn't been signed; the nurse practitioner who had been on duty in the physician's absence had no power to sign for him. So distraught that this development might incriminate his best friend with his mother's murder, Peter suffered a massive stroke. And, in a series of events strongly resembling a Greek tragedy orchestrated by enraged gods, as Peter was slowly recovering, his wife, Caroline, died suddenly of a massive heart attack. "Her heart simply exploded," Porter says.

The physician is convinced that all of these tragic events are connected. "They happened to teach me the limits of what a physician can do," he says. "It was the only physician-assisted death I've taken part in where I actually did the deed, and I knew it was wrong. My mistake with Victoria was that I didn't sit down with her and talk to her about what I was going to do. I didn't find out for myself if she was ready to die, and clearly, she wasn't. So I killed her at the cost of Peter's functional life and Caroline's mortal life. And I learned from it that the limits of a physician's job are 'thou shalt not kill.'"

Porter has never again been—and will never again be—personally responsible for a patient's death, although he continues to believe that under the right circumstances, giving a dying patient the means to kill himself can be the right thing to do. "The purpose is not to be in control of death, but to be able to take charge of it," he says, comparing the difference to that between starving and fasting. "Being in control of something is making it happen, forcing it, whereas being in charge of it involves allowing it to happen and going with the flow of it. If you can learn to let death happen in a way that fits the psychological and spiritual needs of the whole family, then having a physician's expertise can be the right thing to happen."

But he makes a vehement distinction between giving his patients responsibility for their death and doing the deed himself.

"I am convinced now that a fundamental part of the shaman's knowledge is that it is against the law of God to kill anyone, ever," he says. "Acts have consequences. Not in a court of law, but in the life of the soul."

◆ C H A P T E R   1 0 ◆

Rational Suicide
The Password to a New Frontier?

A man who fears suffering is already
suffering from what he fears.
—Montaigne

Should assisted dying become legal, one of the safeguards
that physicians want in place is the assurance that the patient who requests it is mentally competent to decide, and
not propelled by a potentially treatable depression. But
doesn't anyone who is about to die feel some degree of depression? And who decides whether the sadness that they
feel is clouding their judgment or heightening their understanding of their situation?

A growing number of health care workers believe that
the urge to hasten death can be a sane, realistic response to
devastating physical decline. Among particular groups of patients, they say, the demand for hastened death is a common
response. And who are they, these advocates wonder, to dis-

courage such patients from taking a shortcut on their long and difficult road toward death?

The phenomenon that has probably had the most profound effect on a new generation of physicians in the last decade and a half is AIDS, with its relentless spread through communities once unfamiliar with the realities of disease and dying. AIDS has created a new population of generally young patients who have become all too accustomed to living with the specter of death. According to a 1991 study carried out in San Francisco, People With Aids (PWAs) have experienced, on average, the loss of nine friends.

"I've become almost immune to it by now," says 45-year-old Martin Cross, who has lost two lovers to the disease and is now sick with it himself. "I used to be hypersensitive, especially as a Catholic, but now I can be almost unemotional about all the suffering."

The result of all the suffering is a community of people—notably gay men—whose lives have been radicalized and who have learned to demand action and control, notes Howard Grossman, one of the country's leading AIDS physicians and himself an activist who has marched in ACT-UP demonstrations and sat on the board of directors of the Gay Men's Health Crisis. Grossman reports that most of his patients are politically sophisticated health care consumers who demand to have a say in their treatment and, eventually, in the manner of their death. They are a striking contrast to older generations of patients who were brought up to believe that the man in the white coat is a kind of god, whose word is always gospel.

But AIDS has changed many of the rules. "AIDS is a disease which till now had a clear-cut outcome for everyone—they die," Grossman says. "But for many, death takes a long time arriving. In one way or another, all HIV patients come in and say to me, 'I'm not afraid of dying, I'm afraid of the process.'"

Understandably so. People with AIDS tend to die slow and horrible deaths, as they waste away from a variety of AIDS-related cancers, opportunistic infections, and sometimes devastating dementia. According to William Breitbach, M.D., a pain specialist at Memorial Sloan Kettering Hospital, pain among AIDS sufferers is "dramatically undertreated, even in academic centers with a focus on HIV care." In a 1996 study, Breitbach found that, despite their horrible symptoms, only 15 percent of AIDS patients receive enough pain medication.

As a result, the people who have witnessed distressing deaths among their friends are horrified by what they have seen. When PWAs are first diagnosed with HIV, they become terrified by the prospect of the agonizing decline that lies ahead. So they seek out, usually through others within the community, sympathetic physicians who are known to write prescriptions to hasten the end. According to studies, PWAs tend to kill themselves at a rate about 10–20 percent higher than patients suffering from other chronic diseases. And it is probably true that AIDS physicians are more commonly prepared to help their patients to die than those within other specialist groups. A survey published in the *New England*

Journal of Medicine in February 1997 found that, of 118 members of the Bay Area Community Consortium, a group of San Francisco AIDS physicians, 53 percent said they had helped at least one patient to hasten their death. In 1990, the number who made that admission had been 35 percent.

The patients who get professional help are the lucky ones. The majority who can't find, or afford, the "right kind" of physician have to rely on family members or friends, who are often ill-equipped to help them die. When Russell Ogden, a Canadian social worker, conducted a study of assisted deaths among the AIDS population in Vancouver, British Columbia, he found that as many as half the people who tried to kill themselves botched the job, and often brought on themselves even more serious debility and suffering. Their loved ones, in trying to help them die, sometimes resorted to smothering them with pillows, slitting their wrists, even shooting them, in order to end their pain.

Morphine is the most common, and the preferred, way of hastening death, according to a New York nurse who cares for AIDS patients through the final stages of their lives. Despite enormous fears about gruesome suffering at the end of life, he says, very few of his patients actually want to die early. "Most of them are desperate to live, they'll do anything they can to prolong the time they have," the nurse emphasizes. It is only at the very last stages, when the patient is already dying, that family members will sometimes ask him how they can hasten the end. "Depending on what the families have decided, I might show them how to operate the machinery," the nurse says. "But what they do is up to them. It's none of my business, and I want no part of it."

Grossman agrees that, even when they ask for it, death may not always be what these people are seeking. "What they want to know is, will they have some comfort, someone to help them, if they need it?" he says. "Most people will never take advantage of it. The majority, when we help their depression and control their pain, go through the whole process of dying to the end—including many of them who thought they never would. What gives them the strength to do so is the promise that someone will help them end it."

That simple promise, many physicians have noted, is often the best deterrent their patients can have against suicide. When they know they have the means to end suffering should it become unbearable, that knowledge helps them relax, and feel they have a measure of control over their future. Many family members of those who took their lethal drugs say that had their loved one been able to call on a legal means of death, they might have kept going longer. But, afraid that if they waited too long, they would no longer be able to carry it out, they took their own life before their disease was far advanced.

Martin's Japanese lover, Kenji, was one of those who both asked for the control and used it. Kenji was diagnosed with AIDS in 1989 and became very sick very quickly. Martin accompanied him on the difficult journey he had to make to Japan, to inform his family that he was dying. Because the stigma of AIDS would have been too much for his traditional family to bear, he told them he had lung cancer. Only his brother guessed the truth of his disease, and he took it very hard.

"It would have killed his parents to find out, but it was real sad for Kenji to have to keep secrets at that point in his life," Martin says. Still, while they were in Japan, Martin made Kenji's family a solemn promise: that he would bring his companion's cremated remains back to them in person, so that Kenji could be buried in his homeland, among his own ancestors.

Back in the States, Martin gave up his graduate studies to take care of his ailing partner. Kenji, racked by a number of painful infections, decided he wanted to die soon, rather than reach the protracted end stages of his disease. Through the local gay network, Martin helped him find a physician (not his personal physician) who agreed to prescribe him a large amount of morphine—enough to end his life. Then Kenji and Martin plotted how to do the deed.

The plan was for Kenji to hook up the morphine to his intravenous tube, combine it with a dose of Valium, and for good measure, put a plastic bag over his head to help him suffocate if the drug combination didn't work. Because a physician would have to be called to sign the death certificate, the pair worked out a plan to disguise the facts of Kenji's death: He would leave a suicide note in a slightly open drawer in the nightstand. That way, if his death were questioned, Martin could feign discovery of the note, and if it were not, he could simply push the drawer closed. When Kenji prepared to hook up the morphine to his i.v. stand, Martin would leave to pick up a prescription for Kenji at the pharmacy, then call from the street to leave a message on the telephone answering machine, saying he was on his way home. Having established his absence at the time of Kenji's suicide, he would return home to find his companion dead.

Events took place as planned. When Martin returned home, Kenji was lying dead in bed, his i.v. still attached to his arm and a plastic bag over his head, his face beneath it peaceful, with no signs of distress. Despite a lawyer's warning not to touch anything at the bedside, Martin removed the plastic bag and disposed of it. Then he called the hospice under whose care Kenji had been, and they sent around a nurse to help Martin with the final arrangements. "It went so smoothly," Martin recalls. "Everything according to plan."

Sadly for Martin, he was to relive a similar sequence of tragic events 3 years later, when another companion, Stuart, also succumbed to AIDS. Like Kenji, Stuart was given drugs—in his case, barbiturates—from a sympathetic physician, and when he became very ill, but before he was ready to die of natural causes, he took them.

Now, it is Martin's turn to fight the virus. So far, like many AIDS patients these days, a combination of new "protease inhibitor" drugs has made him feel better than he has for years. But he is prepared for whatever may happen further down the road. "I will definitely commit suicide," he says emphatically. "I already have the necessary medications, and they are a tremendous comfort to me—even if I never use them, it's good to know they're there."

Is Martin's decision to stockpile deadly drugs, and his intention to take them when he becomes sick, the sign of depression or of a well-balanced and clear-sighted mind at work? A growing number of health care professionals—mainly psychiatric social workers and counselors—who have worked a lot with dying patients, believe that the desire to commit suicide among those who are terminally ill and suffering can be an utterly rational response.

The term "rational suicide" is a relatively new one in the expanding lexicon of the right-to-die movement. But can there really be such a thing? Opponents fervently believe that "rational suicide" is a contradiction in terms: that suicide, by definition, is an irrational act that can be inspired only by some form of temporary or longstanding mental imbalance, most frequently by depression.

"Depression is the single factor found to be a significant predictor of the desire for death," claims the American Medical Association in its "amicus" brief to the Supreme Court. And it quotes a study from the *New England Journal of Medicine* "Of 44 patients in the end stages of cancer, only three had considered suicide and each of them had a severe clinical depression."

"In our experience, patients who ask for death are depressed, even if they deny it," says the AMA's Reardon. And if they're depressed, Reardon says, they can be treated; with counseling and the correct antidepressants, the wish to die almost always disappears.

One of those who is skeptical about that claim is James Werth, Ph.D., who was a staff clinician at the University of Arkansas's Counselling and Psychological Services when he wrote *Rational Suicide? Implications for Mental Health Professionals.*

"From my perspective, the cornerstone issue in the right-to-die debate is whether a patient's desire for death is rational or not," Werth says. "For me, the entire argument rests on whether a person is able to make a rational choice. Any talk of assisted suicide is premature until that's been decided."

Werth says he came by his beliefs gradually, through working with AIDS patients in hospitals, where he saw terrible pain and suffering, without any hope of alleviation or recovery. "I was taught always to discourage suicide when I came across it in my work," he says. "But after a while, I began to question that. I started to think, Why is it irrational to want to hasten death when one is so ill and has no hope of recovery or release from suffering?"

Werth conducted a study to see whether other psychologists shared his opinion. The study, published in the summer of 1995 in the journal *Suicide and Life Threatening Behavior,* showed that of the more than 200 psychologists surveyed, 81 percent believed in the notion of rational suicide. They even offered criteria whereby they might consider a plea for death to be a well-measured response. From their answers, Werth distilled a set of guidelines to help others formulate such a conclusion. Some of them are criteria already agreed to by physicians: that the patient has "an unremittingly hopeless physical condition"; that she has made her decision as a free choice, without pressure from others; that the patient has considered all of the alternatives, and thought about the impact of her act on her loved ones. But other criteria are more unorthodox: that the patient has talked with objective others such as medical professionals, clergy, and, in particular, a mental health professional who is qualified to assess psychological competence.

The idea of rational suicide has already gained a foothold within the psychiatric community. As far back as 1993, the National Association of Social Workers made a policy statement that their members should be able to participate in helping people who have made a rational choice to commit suicide, by referring them to a physician sympathetic to their point of view. "I believe mental health professionals have a major role to play in helping decrease the opposition to hastened death," says Werth. "Physicians don't spend time assessing the criteria of what might make the request for death a rational choice, but I think that's part of a mental health worker's job."

If it is, it is nonetheless difficult and controversial work, as the mental health of a patient, particularly one contemplating death, is far more quixotic and hard to gauge than his physical health is likely to be. "After all, what does rational really mean?" asks psychiatrist Herbert Hendin, executive director of the American Suicide Foundation. "Rational people can disagree about all kinds of things, particularly over premises and values. And even if, in a particular situation, someone were to make a rational decision to end their life, that doesn't make it a justification for basing social policy on it, it simply makes that particular case rational."

So how do we judge? Consider the case of quadriplegic Larry McAfee, who sought and won the right to die in court, only to go on to experience a new lease on life, and to die of natural causes 4 years later.

Twenty-nine-year-old McAfee, from Atlanta, Georgia, was catastrophically injured in May 1985, when his motorcycle, traveling at no more than 10 mph, skidded on a curve on a mountain road. McAfee was thrown off, and the base of his helmet crushed the top two vertebrae of his spine. He sustained what is called a "complete injury"—one that left him utterly paralyzed from the neck down, unable to move, eat, or even breathe without the help of a respirator.

McAfee's parents were unable to look after him or to afford the around-the-clock care he needed. So for 4 years, he was shunted from one institution to the next, from Georgia to Ohio to Alabama, in search of a facility that would keep him. Some couldn't because his nursing needs exceeded their capacity; others weren't covered by insurance; still others sent him away because they couldn't cope with his abusive rage. He was disgusted by his surroundings, bitter, hopeless, and deeply depressed. "You're just a sack of potatoes," he said about himself.

In 1989, he applied to a Georgia Superior Court for the right to kill himself. The judge granted his request and ruled that McAfee's physicians could prescribe him deadly drugs, to be administered via an intravenous tube that McAfee himself would be able to control. McAfee designed a switch that he could operate himself and that would release the drugs whenever he wanted them. He had said that he didn't want his ventilator disconnected (which also would have killed him) because he was afraid to die by suffocation.

The switch McAfee had designed was installed. But at the eleventh hour, a stranger came forward who was to persuade him to give life another chance.

Russ Fine, Ph.D., was the director of the Injury Prevention Research Center at the University of Alabama in Birmingham. He had read about McAfee's legal struggles in the local press and, haunted by the case, decided to contact him. After several rebuffed attempts, McAfee finally agreed to meet Fine. The physician drove the 25 miles to the nursing home in a state of anxious anticipation.

"I walked into the two-bed ward, and there was no one in the other bed, just Larry, glaring at the ceiling," Fine recalls. "He had nothing to say, so I started talking—and talking. I said I knew things had been bad, but I felt fate had thrown us together and I was willing to do what I could for him if he'd just give me a chance."

Eventually, Fine's persistence and optimism wore McAfee down; the quadriplegic agreed to allow Fine to prove to him that life could be worth living, on the condition that, if he could not, he would help McAfee trigger his switch. Fine agreed.

The first thing Fine did was to make some changes to McAfee's living conditions. He had been horrified to find that there was no television or radio in his room, no voice-activated telephone—nothing to stimulate him or distract him from himself. Fine quickly raised some money among friends and colleagues, and bought him some machines to make life more bearable. Then he and his wife, Dee, began visiting McAfee regularly—during the day or late in the evenings after Fine finished work. On holidays, the couple would bring in special meals and treats. Fine remembers one Thanksgiving in particular, when McAfee reached an important turning point.

"I had brought lunch to the nursing home and after lunch, I crawled up onto his bed and got sleepy lying there, watching the football game, with Larry next to me in his wheelchair," Fine recalls. "Suddenly, I realized that Larry had gone into acute respiratory distress—he was suffocating and turning black. I rang the bell and got an orderly. The two of us pulled back his wheelchair so he was tilted back, and the therapist started bagging him while I began pounding on his chest. We resuscitated him and brought him back upright. I was trembling and perspiring, but I suddenly noticed that Larry was weeping. I said to him, 'Are you crying because you didn't die?' and Larry gasped, 'No, I was scared.' I knew then that he didn't want to die. But he didn't want to live as he had been living—his life was horrible. So we began working doubly hard to make some changes."

"We," of course, meant Fine and his wife, who despite their own demanding jobs and family, spent hours working on McAfee's behalf. In the summer of 1989, Fine persuaded officials at Birmingham's United Cerebral Palsy to let him move temporarily into one of their group homes for the severely disabled. McAfee thrived at the home and was bitterly disappointed when he was forced to leave because of lack of funding. But as a result of media interest in his case, the Medical College of Georgia created an independent living facility for McAfee and five other patients. He was living there when he suffered the first of a series of strokes that, in 1995, killed him.

Because of his devotion and persistence, Russ Fine brought several important changes into McAfee's life. Not just the friendship and company that McAfee had so lacked, but also the energy to fight for the disabled man's rights and improved living conditions. In interviews before his death, McAfee spoke of the factors that had prompted him to reverse his decision to die. The first, he said, was having the freedom to live an independent life. "If I ever have to return to an institution, then I prefer death," he said. But he also spoke of the switch that he had had put in place. He never dismantled it, and said that it gave him a sense of "control"—something that up until that point he had utterly lacked. It is the same sense of control that other patients report feeling when they have managed to stockpile deadly drugs or have secured a promise of help from a friend, or, better yet, a physician: The knowledge that suffering does not have to be indefinite brings with it enormous relief.

*   *   *

McAfee's case begs many questions from both sides of the argument. Opponents say that had he enacted his right to die immediately, he would never have met Russ Fine, nor consequently experienced the friendship, empowerment, and new sense of life's possibilities that Fine brought with him.

Proponents counter that very few people in McAfee's position come across people like Russ Fine. Instead, they languish in substandard nursing homes, suffering neglect and misery, as he did for 4 long years, and are never bailed out. What's more, they say, at a time of dramatically shrinking health care resources, there are likely to be more, not fewer, McAfees left to vegetate in deplorable conditions. Failing acceptable alternatives, why shouldn't these people, if they find those conditions unbearable, be able to choose an escape?

Russ Fine, who says he opposes the notion of assisted death, says he nonetheless always believed in McAfee's right to end his life. "I didn't want him to, but I always supported his right to get out if that's what he wanted to do," Fine says. He also believes that people can decide rationally that they no longer want to live. "I believe there are things worse than death," he says. "I could see that one might not want to live without a decent quality of life." Fine believes that McAfee made his decision to die rationally; and rationally, he also realized that his life could improve.

Having worked among people who have sustained disastrous injuries, Fine says he has seen time and again that once they get over the initial shock of what has happened,

"Ninety percent decide there is a life afterwards. Very few people kill themselves or want to die." Still, his experiences with McAfee made him realize just how vulnerable disabled people are to a law permitting the right to die. "They have every reason to feel threatened," he says. "There *is* a slippery slope, and there's no reason to rush there. Sometimes it's the families who'd be relieved if the person were to die. I'm afraid there would be coercion if the opportunity was there."

◆ C H A P T E R   1 1 ◆

Suspicion and Fear
from the Vulnerable

The remedy is worse than the disease.
—Francis Bacon

On January 8, 1997, a group of disabled people in wheelchairs and vans, dragging along ventilators and attached to
colostomy bags, assembled on the steps of the U.S. Supreme
Court in Washington to let the country know that they were
Not Dead Yet. Nor were they planning to be anytime soon:
Their presence at the courthouse was intended to demon-
strate their fervent opposition to the right-to-die legislation
that the Court was scheduled to start debating that day.

"We're very afraid that assisted suicide isn't going to be
made available only to the terminally ill," says Diane Coleman, a founding member of Not Dead Yet. "The courts have
frequently decided that the lives of disabled people are
'meaningless.' Well, they're not to us."

In the short time that this activist group has been in existence, it has already made its angry presence felt. Not Dead Yet started off its campaign in June 1996 in front of the Michigan home of Dr. Kevorkian, where members protested his involvement in the death of Bette Lou Hamilton the day before. Hamilton was a 67-year-old woman with a degenerative spinal disease, one of more than a dozen patients who were not terminally ill that the doctor has helped to die. Since then, Not Dead Yet has "gatecrashed" a bioethical conference in Michigan, protested at the Denver headquarters of the Hemlock Society, set up its own website, infiltrated the right-to-die mailing list with its "manifesto" and the angry comments of numerous persistent members, spoke before a congressional committee, and submitted an "amicus" brief to the Supreme Court. The brief says, in part:

"People with disabilities have already been endangered by relaxation of laws and policies protecting their lives. Medical rehabilitation specialists report that quadriplegics and other significantly disabled people are dying wrongfully in increasing numbers because emergency room physicians judge their quality of life as low and, therefore, withhold aggressive treatment." According to Coleman, a number of disabled people who are treated in emergency rooms are told that, whether they have filled in "do not resuscitate" orders or not, they will not be resuscitated, as medical staff do not consider the cost or the effort worthwhile.

Coleman, who has a neuromuscular disorder called spinal muscular atrophy, conducts her busy life (she is also executive director of the Progress Center for Independent Living in Oak Park, Illinois) from a motorized wheelchair. "I have been working for more than a decade to bring the perspective of disabled people to the public, the medical establishment and the media," she says. The perspective is, quite simply, that despite their severe physical problems, disabled people want to be alive—and would want life all the more if society took their needs, physical and emotional, into greater account.

"Our perspective is permanently ignored, we're simply not included in the debate," Coleman concludes. "People claim that this law is only for the terminally ill. It isn't. But this train is moving so fast, no one's looking to see what's really happening."

Around the country, as the right-to-die movement's agenda gains a stronger foothold, disabled people, the relatives of patients in comatose or vegetative states, the chronically ill, and even the elderly, are increasingly frightened about what a law legalizing physician aid in dying could mean for them. They point to a dramatic 1998 Canadian case as an example of their worst fears: that others will decide for them whether their lives are worth living or not.

The case involved Robert Latimer, a 42-year-old farmer who one morning ended the life of his 12-year-old daughter, Tracy, while the rest of his family was in church. Tracy had been born with severe cerebral palsy and was unable to walk, feed herself, or talk. She also experienced acute pain from a displaced hip. But, as the prosecution pointed out, the pain wasn't continuous, and physicians believed they could operate to make it more bearable. What's more, the attorney argued, Tracy had never asked her parents to help her die.

Latimer admitted killing Tracy. He felt she was suffering unbearably, had always suffered unbearably, and he had acted to end her suffering. He had carried her to the front seat of his pickup truck, fed in a hosepipe, and filled the truck with exhaust fumes. But Latimer's jury, despite finding him guilty of second-degree murder, requested that the court not impose the mandatory minimum sentence of 10 years behind bars. For the first time in a Canadian murder case, the judge allowed a constitutional exemption to lighten the punishment. Latimer was eventually given a 2-year sentence, with just 1 year to be served in jail. While his supporters considered the judge in the case, Justice Ted Noble of the Saskatchewan Court of Queen's Bench, to be an "ethical pioneer" for his decision, opponents were horrified. "This says it's OK for a parent to murder a child with a disability," said one disabled group spokesman. Said another: "To exempt people who kill us from the consequences of their murders—based on the assertion of compassion as motivation—is to put every disabled person at great risk."

The disabled aren't the only ones who fear being put at risk. Those who report feeling threatened by society's alleged growing tolerance of assisted death also include women, minorities, and poor people—those who lack financial resources and social clout, and who believe they are never given *enough* treatment, and therefore don't even consider the possibility that they might be given too much. Also feeling vulnerable are the elderly. In a recent survey of 168 frail old people (average age 76 years) carried out at the Geriatric Evaluation and Treatment Center at Duke University Medical Center in Durham, North Carolina, researchers found that 40 percent of them were in favor of physician-assisted death for terminally ill patients. By contrast, among 146 of their spouses, siblings, and children, the percentage in favor was 59.6. The survey also found that the relatives were not very good at predicting how their elderly relatives felt about physician-assisted death. This is a significant finding given that these are the people who would have to step in and make a medical decision were their relative to become unable to make his or her decision known.

Duke psychiatrist Harold Koenig, M.D., the leading investigator in the study, said he found the results to be "of great concern because the frail elderly, poorly educated and demented members of our society have little power to influence public policy that may directly affect them." Koenig added that if physician assisted suicide were to be made legal, this vulnerable population "may warrant special protective measures."

As just such a measure, Earl Appleby, a disabled rights activist, founded a patients-rights group called CURE, Citizens United to Resist Euthanasia. "My conclusion is that 80 percent of patients die because they're not given elective treatment, either because their quality of life isn't considered good enough to begin with, or because of financial reasons," he says.

Appleby speaks from personal experience. In 1981, his father fell into an irreversible coma. He had suffered a heart attack at home, then a second one when he arrived at the hospital. His heart stopped beating and in the half-hour that it took to resuscitate him, a lack of oxygen to the brain induced the coma.

"The physician said there was a 95 percent chance he'd die, but he survived," Appleby says. Because of the serious nature of his condition, the Appleby family found that the hospital was reluctant to treat him. "They felt it was futile because he'd never come out of his coma," he said. "We had to fight very vigorously to get him the treatment we felt he needed."

Eventually, after 6 months in the hospital, his condition was deemed stable enough for the Applebys to bring him home. They cared for him there for 9 years, until his death in 1990. "Those years were very precious to us," Appleby says.

It was as a result of what the family had to go through to assure their father of the treatment he needed that Appleby and his mother began CURE. Appleby says that CURE's aims are not political; they do not lobby for their cause or protest publicly.

"We're philosophically opposed to euthanasia but we don't twist people's arms," he says. What he and his family do is simply to try to help families in situations similar to their own. And that is full-time work, he says, because there are a lot of families nationwide who find themselves in such a position: Appleby claims they're contacted by two or three each month.

"It's difficult enough to face the crisis of disease, but disease is a part of life," he says. "What's unconscionable is when there's a constant stream of negativity foisted on the family by the physician and others. That is simply cruelty."

One of the families CURE claims to have helped was Helga and Oliver Wanglie, an elderly couple from Minneapolis who, in 1991, got embroiled in a precedent-setting court case against the hospital that wanted to discontinue Helga Wanglie's treatment.

Helga Wanglie was 86 years old when she tripped on a rug in her home and fell, breaking her hip. After an initially good recovery, she developed various complications, was put on a respirator, and then had a heart attack that left her with irreversible brain damage. Physicians pronounced her to be in a persistent vegetative state, with no hope of recovery. They suggested to her 89-year-old husband that they stop the intensive measures they had been taking to keep her alive.

Mrs. Wanglie had no living will, but her husband insisted that as a devout Lutheran, she had told him she wanted every possible measure taken to save her life. The rest of her family agreed, hoping for a miracle. After trying in vain to change the family's mind, the hospital took the unprecedented step of taking the case to court, where they asked for the appointment of an independent guardian. Oliver Wanglie, a retired lawyer, fought back by bringing his own suit, demanding that he be made his wife's guardian.

At the first hearing, the presiding judge ruled for the hospital, saying that "physicians have a duty to overrule families in certain circumstances. I believe a doctor cannot be obligated and should not be obligated to provide medical care which cannot serve a patient's personal, medical interest."

But at appeal, a different judge gave the guardianship of Helga Wanglie to her husband. Three days later, the then 87-year-old woman died, leaving behind a medical bill of more than $750,000.

Appleby shudders at the mention of medical costs. He is a firm believer that "the drive toward coercive mass euthanasia," which is what he believes the right-to-die movement really is, is fueled in large part by cost consideration. Because of the enormous expense of health care today, Appleby thinks more people are being undertreated than overtreated—a situation he feels can only get worse. "Managed care is a form of checkbook euthanasia," he says. "It's more economical not to be treated. My father was a veteran and he cost the Veterans Administration a lot of money, which they probably didn't want to spend. Other people have to pay their own medical costs. And what a terrible thing to be made to feel that because of cost, you're a burden on your family."

Ironically, Herbert Hendin, executive director of the National Suicide Foundation and a firm opponent of assisted death, notes that while euthanasia is undoubtedly a cheaper option than sophisticated medical intervention or long-term palliative care, legalizing it may end up a lot more expensive than Americans imagine—mainly because U.S. physicians, living in the most litigious society in the world, can expect a tremendous number of lawsuits to result from helping their patients to die.

"The doctors who support this legalization don't understand what they're asking for," Hendin says. "Prosecutors in this country won't be as benevolent as they are in the Netherlands."

The different factions that have come together to oppose physician-assisted death make up an interesting and unconventional alliance. This coalition is less homogeneous and less politically conservative than the antiabortion movement. It brings together those who believe in abortion and those who do not, those who are religiously motivated and those who are not, those who consider themselves "liberals" as well as their conservative brethren, and those who fight from their living rooms alongside representatives of mighty institutions.

The two mightiest institutions that have put their formidable lobbying powers behind defeating right-to-die legalization are the Catholic Church, which is vehemently opposed to ending life under any circumstance, and the National Right-to-Life movement, whose organizational skills have been honed by years of antiabortion conflict. So far, right-to-life protestors have only rarely used aggressive picketing techniques to fight physician aid in dying. One of their tactics was allegedly to "slander and humiliate" Cheryl Gale, the widow of one of Kevorkian's patients, Hugh Gale, who died in 1993. Mrs. Gale won an appeal in the Michigan Court of Appeals to pursue damages against three right-to-life groups—Operation Rescue, Advocates for Life, and the Christian Defense Coalition—for allegedly causing her emotional distress with accusations that she assisted and consented to her husband's unlawful death. But such incidents are rare; by and large, the opposition groups have directed their considerable clout toward demonstrating their dissent on a more wide-reaching scale. Burke Baulch, director of the department of medical ethics at the National Right to Life Committee, refuses to reveal his organization's vision for the fight ahead: "It's not our policy to discuss the strategy of our ongoing campaigns," he says. He is, however, more than willing to rattle off, at breathless speed, his organization's ethical arguments against assisted death, and declares that, following the Supreme Court ruling, the anticipated tussle of numerous individual state legislations to fashion their own laws over the next few years "will be fought out at a high pitch of intensity." Baulch adds, "There is no question that the struggle over euthanasia will be one of the most dominant issues into the next century."

The Catholic Church agrees. Representing more than 60 million followers, the largest religious group in the United States, the Church has been fighting assisted suicide at a number of levels, from the Pope himself, who frequently censures what he calls "the culture of death," to its lowly representatives in parishes across the country.

Despite its unbending denunciations, the Church's teachings recognize differences between euthanasia, which it considers to be murder, and the withholding or refusal of treatment, which the Church permits in cases where it is clear that medical intervention will either be futile or prolong suffering. Catholics also support the right to administer pain medication to dying patients, even while acknowledging the possible "double effect."

"It is licit to relieve pain by narcotics, even when the result is decreased consciousness and a shortening of life," allows no less an authority than Pope John Paul II, in his 1995 encyclical, "The Gospel of Life." But the ostensible purpose must be to relieve pain. Only then is it acceptable to tinker with the natural process of dying. In 1998, the Pope reiterated his beliefs in a terse admonition that pain relief must not be administered for ulterior motives, such as speeding death.

Across the country, priests have been instructed to give sermons condemning the legalization of assisted death, and emphasizing the spiritual importance of accepting suffering. In Detroit, on the home turf of Dr. Kevorkian, the Catholic community is working hard to provide its people with alternatives to the physician's services when it comes to their end-of-life decisions. Adam Cardinal Maida, who presides over the archdiocese's 1.4 million Catholics, was asked by the National Conference of Bishops to "keep the point position on this," according to one of his assistants. To do so, the archdiocese has set up Project Life, a telephone hotline available 24 hours a day to offer callers other options to abortion or ending their life. According to spokesman Howard Haflein, the hotline has received hundreds of calls since it was set up in July 1996, from people wanting to help as well as from those asking for help. In matters of death and dying, Haflein says, their calls are referred to Detroit's Angela Hospice.

The Catholic Church has also committed a huge amount of money to defeating assisted death legislation. In Washington State in 1991 and in California the following year, local Catholic organizations ran elaborate propaganda campaigns against the aid-in-dying propositions, totaling almost $2 million and $4 million, respectively. The money was spent on mailing information packages to every parish, encouraging Masses for the dead and volunteers at hospices. Large sums were also spent on advertising. In the 1997 Oregon campaign to repeal the assisted dying legislation, the state's powerful Catholic lobby invested $4 million, most of it to underwrite a major media blitz that they kicked off weeks before their adversaries, whom they outspent threefold.

Curiously, despite their well-orchestrated campaign, the opposition was less successful the second time, when post-election analysis indicated that no more than 20 percent of voters were ultimately influenced by partisan propaganda. At the start of the 1994 campaign, polls had shown that a majority of the populace—Catholics and non-Catholics alike—were in favor of the proposition. By the end, after weeks of persuasive television and media advertising, 82 percent of churchgoing Catholics and 60 percent of all Catholics in the state voted against the proposition.

Probably the most effective spokesman the Catholic Church has had in opposing physician aid in dying has been

Joseph Cardinal Bernadin, Chicago's Roman Catholic archbishop, who died in November 1996 at the age of 68, after losing a year-long battle with pancreatic cancer. Bernadin, who
initially thought that surgery had cured him, was told just a
few months later that his cancer had spread to his liver and
was inoperable. Almost from the beginning, he decided to inform the public of his condition, and he kept them aware of
his final journey right until its end. After years of fearing
death, as he admitted, Bernadin used his last months to confront those fears, and also to campaign against assisted suicide. Literally days before he died, the Cardinal submitted a
letter via the Catholic Health Association to the Supreme
Court, asking them not to make the practice legal.

"As one who is dying, I have especially come to appreci-
ate the gift of life," Bernadin wrote. He explained that he felt
the issue was not simply a private matter between a patient
and his physician, but rather, an important public one. "Our
legal and ethical tradition has held consistently that suicide,
assisted-suicide, and euthanasia are wrong because they involve a direct attack on innocent human life," Bernadin
wrote. "Creating a new right to assisted suicide will endanger society and send a false signal that a less than 'perfect'
life is not worth living."

Who gets to decide whose life is less than perfect? Opponents
fear that, with the sanction of the courts, legalized aid in dying will give physicians—not patients—the increased powers
to make those choices. And their deepest, most pervasive fear

is that, if that becomes so, the parameters of what's accept-able will expand—until physicians are helping chronically ill patients as well as fatally ill ones, those whose suffering is mental as well as physical, and finally those who, no matter what they themselves think, are deemed to have a quality of life so poor that it's not worth saving. At the end of a century in which the memory of the gruesome Nazi eugenics program casts an indelible shadow, it is not surprising that its recol-lection still causes reverberations.

The fears begin with the fact that not only was the Ger-man eugenics movement underway long before World War II, but that it was professional psychiatrists and pediatricians, not Nazis, who first launched the program that killed 75 per-cent of Germany's chronically ill population, snatched from hospitals, nursing homes, and asylums. And as the killing picked up speed, the victims became progressively less dis-abled, until it was enough to have "badly modeled ears" or to be "difficult to educate."

Chillingly, the truth is that the murderous impulses that ended the lives of those estimated 100,000 Germans did not exist exclusively within Germany's borders: In the Nether-lands, the early euthanasia debate was informed by eugenic considerations. And in Sweden, for over 40 years, until as late as 1976, physicians sterilized more than 60,000 people, mainly poor, young women and "weak" people, with the in-tention of reducing the national welfare program and, in the process, creating a better species. France, Denmark, Norway, and Switzerland have also admitted having had forms of such eugenics programs, albeit on a smaller scale than Sweden. In the light of dramatic increases in aging populations, inadequate nursing home care, and rising medical costs, several European politicians admit that they share concerns with Dutch euthanasia proponent Dr. Pieter Admiraal, who thinks that, in 25 years, Europe may resort to euthanasia to deal with the problem of its swelling population of old people.

The United States has also had its share of eugenics enthusiasts.

"Proponents of physician-assisted suicide are offended when allusions are made to this piece of disability history in the course of debate over the so-called 'right to die,'" claims Steven N. Drake, a member of Not Dead Yet. "The fact is that Hitler stole most of his ideas on eugenics from publications originating in the USA."

One of the earliest known American proponents of eugenics was Harry J. Haiselden, a Chicago surgeon who believed in ridding the world of the "army of unfit" who, as "horrid semi-humans," had "lives of no value." Between 1915 and 1918, Haiselden allowed or hastened the death of at least six deformed babies, one of whom he let bleed to death. Haiselden campaigned vigorously for his cause in the news media, at conferences, and even in a 1916 silent movie, *The Black Stork,* named for the evil stork that delivered disfigured babies. His campaign drew support from such unlikely figures as Helen Keller, the blind and deaf advocate for the disabled, and the venerated lawyer Clarence Darrow. After his early death in 1919, Haiselden was practically written out of American history, until author Martin Pernick, a historian at the University of Michigan, discovered the only surviving print of his film, and wrote a book about Haiselden's life, *The Black Stork.*

There have been other American eugenics supporters. In Derek Humphry and Ann Wickett's historical overview, *The Right to Die,* the authors quote from "Should They Live?," a 1938 publication written by William G. Lennox.

"If we are farsighted, we shall begin to do something about that portion of our population which is a heavy and permanent liability," Lennox wrote. "Congenital idiots or monsters . . . incurably sick with heart, joint or lung disease. . . . In the betterment of race, medicine must play a part. . . . One of the guiding posts: The privilege of death for the congenitally mindless and for the incurably sick who wish to die."

Activist Drake says that the desire for such solutions is not a thing of the past. He quotes from a 1983 study in the journal *Pediatrics.* The study, which was performed at Oklahoma Children's Memorial Hospital, used a "quality of life" formula to decide whether to give parents of infants with spina bifida an "optimistic" or a "pessimistic" prognosis. Parents given an optimistic prognosis were informed of the available treatments and encouraged to begin them immediately. All complied. The parents of children given a "pessimistic" prognosis were told that their children were too disabled to ever be able to enjoy life should they survive, and were recommended to forego intervention or treatment. Most parents, having been told this was in their children's best in-

terests, obliged. According to the report, "The 'untreated survivor' has not been a significant problem in our experience.
All 24 babies who have not been treated at all have died at an
average of 37 days." Meanwhile, 3 out of 5 of the babies who
were given treatment were alive and doing well when the article was written. This fact drew Steven Drake to conclude
that "there is a ready acceptance of the physician's 'duty' to
judge the quality of life of patients, to deem when it will be
unacceptable, and to act as executioner when it is felt to be
desirable according to professionally determined criteria."
Drake concludes: "None of the current debate is really new. It
just took 50 years to come back out in the open."

But out in the open it now is, they fear. And to prove it,
they point to a statement that Dr. Kevorkian made in a
Michigan courtroom in 1990.

"The voluntary self-elimination of individual mortally
diseased or crippled lives, taken collectively, can only en-
hance the preservation of public health and welfare."

To advocates, the opposition's fears may seem extreme.
Kevorkian's lawyer, Geoffrey Fieger, believes that interpret-
ing his client's words as a call for a modern eugenics movement is the reaction not of the physically disabled but of "the
mentally disabled and one of their disabilities includes para-
noia." Yet protestors are quick to point out that, even without
laws to sanction his actions, almost half of the people
Kevorkian has helped to die have not been terminally ill.
Three, according to the Oakland County medical examiner,
had no physical illness at all. And one, according to his med-

ical records, had a history of mental illness and may not have been competent to make a rational decision.

There are any number of reasons why these people may have chosen to die, reasons that are surely unconnected with anyone's wish to curtail en masse the lives of particular groups of people. But, according to opponents of assisted suicide, there are many possible solutions to their suffering, other than being helped to die. Antidepressant medication, comfort care for pain, and the ability to talk to a supportive physician are all options that could give a suicidal patient a different outcome: a natural death. That, they say, is the true definition of death with dignity.

CHAPTER 12

Religion and Ethics
Who Cares for the Soul?

In the midst of life we are in death.
—The Book of Common Prayer

Dying, according to the Reverend Kenneth Phifer, is a spiritual matter—a time when the power of medicine has reached its limit and when physicians should withdraw to allow for the care of the soul. Yet when physicians and hospital administrators, along with lawyers and politicians, are all so busy arguing over the rights and wrongs of assisted dying, who is there to care for the soul?

Traditionally, of course, that is the job of the clergy. It is a great irony that, despite the fact that most religions are constructed around interpretations of death and the possibility of an afterlife, very few religious figures are engaged in the battle over the right to die. In this country, the battle is being framed in medical and legal terms, rather than in spiritual or religious ones.

America, however, does have a long tradition of church leaders who have drawn their congregants into political confrontations: over the Vietnam War and the civil rights movement; over nuclear disarmament and the need to end poverty and the suffering of hunger. Today, terminally ill people who are dying lingering, unaided deaths are suffering horribly. Yet those community leaders assigned to the care of our immortal souls are either deeply opposed to physician aid in dying, or as unwilling to tackle it as the rest of the country: ambivalent and undecided, reluctant to make waves.

Phifer is frustrated by his colleagues' absence in the debate. "I'm disappointed that the issue is continually shoved into the medical realm when dying is a time when people need their spiritual counselors by their side," he says.

Phifer has tried to provide this presence for his own congregants. In 1993, he accompanied parishioner Merian Frederick on her one-way journey to see Dr. Kevorkian. Frederick was suffering from the agonizing progression of Lou Gehrig's disease and Kevorkian had offered her the quick and easy way of dying that she wanted. She asked Phifer to be with her at her death, and as her priest, he had no hesitation. Nevertheless, as the senior minister of the First Universalist Unitarian Church in Ann Arbor, Michigan, Phifer knew that abetting a parishioner in receiving physician-assisted suicide was not just illegal but, for a minister in particular, a highly contentious action. Still, he decided that whatever the personal cost, he was going to be by her side.

A few days before they were scheduled to leave, Phifer telephoned his superior and told him "an event" was about to happen that would bring attention—possible adverse attention—to the church. In anticipation, he proffered his resignation. It was refused. What's more, the church's board of trustees promised Phifer their support. Today, the Universalist Unitarian Association, which represents more than 1000 congregations in the United States and Canada, is one of the most vociferous supporters of assisted dying within the religious community. In 1988, it adopted a resolution asserting "the right to self-determination in dying, and the release from civil and criminal penalties of those who, under proper safeguards, act to honor the right of terminally ill patients to select the time of their own deaths."

Kenneth Phifer is an unusual minister for many reasons, not least for his attitude to assisted dying. He is devoted to his parishioners and goes to great lengths to give them the spiritual guidance they crave. He tries not to judge, or to impose a religious or moral code on them. "Personal autonomy is a profoundly important part of human life, and of our faith," he says. "I believe each person has the right to make their own decision about their life, and autonomy is the right to say, 'I've suffered enough.'"

Once Merian Frederick learned that Kevorkian was willing to help her, she became less afraid of the disease that was rapidly spreading through her, and grew more relaxed. She was able to enjoy the last weeks of her life, Phifer says, because "she knew there was a terminal point to her suffering."

When the date of her appointment with Kevorkian arrived, Phifer and one of Frederick's daughters drove her across the state to the appointed place. They left in the dead of night, at 4.30 AM, so as not to alert friends or the press. Just 3 hours later, Merian Frederick was dead. Phifer's only sense of sadness was that, afterwards, Kevorkian told him that he had been the first religious leader to have attended such a death. "Merian was the 19th person he had helped to die," Phifer says. "That's a devastating commentary."

Reverend Lawrence Falkowski, Ph.D., rector of the Holy Trinity Episcopal Church in West Orange, New Jersey, agrees. He too feels strongly that religious figures have a duty to get involved with the issue of physician-assisted dying, whether they feel comfortable about it or not. "There is not a religion I know of that doesn't have to deal with life and death issues, but many clergy today are as happy to avoid end-of-life issues as doctors are," Falkowski says. "If the church ignores these issues on a routine basis, then the value of the church goes down. If you sanitize and homogenize all these religious messages, then religion itself becomes an artifact instead of a living, breathing philosophy."

For Falkowski, the jump into activism took place in 1995, at the urging of his superior, the Rt. Rev. John S. Spong, bishop of the Episcopal diocese of Newark, New Jersey. Spong asked Falkowski to cochair a special task force to examine the important emerging issue of physician-assisted dying within the context of the Episcopal Church. One of the most intricate issues requiring investigation was the connection Christians make between faith and suffering, based on the Passion of Christ and its redemptive effect on mankind. Virtually every Christian denomination has its own interpretation of the spiritual value of pain. However, New Jersey's Episcopal Task Force concluded that enduring suffering cannot be taken as a mandate—either theological or moral.

"It is not a moral failing to view such suffering as devoid of purpose, and thus without redemptive value," the task force wrote. "This, coupled with a clear precedent of Jesus' countless efforts to alleviate suffering through His healing ministry, makes clear that there is no obligation incumbent upon the Christian to endure suffering for its own sake."

To a point, even modern Catholics believe this view today. Although the Catholic Church remains the most vocal opponent of hastening death, insisting that pain is the vital connection between believers and Christ's agony on the Cross, some forms of compromise are deemed acceptable. For example, the church supports the removal of life-sustaining technology when it is shown to be ineffective, as well as the withholding of food, water, and medication. It also permits pain medication to be given to a patient whose suffering is unbearable, even if that medication eventually leads to the "double effect": death. The difference, Catholics explain, is one of intent: Administering large doses of pain medication is intended to alleviate suffering, not to shorten life.

Although Phifer regards this view as "moral hypocrisy," he respects the Catholic Church for addressing the issue of assisted death. "They have taken the issue with the utmost seriousness, and have done an excellent job at putting their position before the community," he says. No one would argue. The Catholic position is that physician-assisted death is a form of murder, and should be opposed at all costs. As a result, in every state where hastened death has appeared on the ballot, Catholics have been there, running well-coordinated and heavily financed campaigns against it. Vatican representatives have issued public condemnations of every international right-to-die development, from the first legal assisted deaths in Australia in 1996, to the U.S. Supreme Court deliberations early in 1997. And major Catholic philosophers, such as Richard Doerflinger, a policy expert for the National Conference of Catholic Bishops' Secretariat for Pro-Life Activities, have engaged actively in the debate, at conferences, in print and in the national media. "It is religion's role to remind society of both the value of life and of death," Doerflinger told the *New York Times Magazine* (July 21, 1996).

Some would argue that it is also religion's role to help believers deal with the changing social developments that affect the value of life and death. For example, critics point out that almost 6 months after Oregon passed its right-to-die law, the Catholic community was still busy attacking it, rather than working with the medical community to draw up workable guidelines and safeguards. "I have not seen a single commentary by a religious figure in Oregon," says an observer of the law's progression. "The only guidelines that exist are offered by health professionals or blue-ribbon panels of doctors, lawyers, and ethicists. Where will people turn for their emotional support?"

There are many ways that the clergy can—and should—be involved in the debate, from helping form policy and addressing public meetings to giving sermons from the pulpit, and perhaps most important of all, allowing parishioners to openly discuss the option with them, privately or within study groups. There are some who do, but they are a distinct minority: the Episcopal diocese of Washington, which arranged a task force to examine the issue and ended up unable to reach a consensus, has nonetheless agreed to keep the discussions going. The Rev. Andrew Short, a Presbyterian minister from Austin, Texas, deeply affected by the prolonged suffering of his cancer-stricken wife, joined the board of the Hemlock Society in order to add a religious perspective to the group, and to counsel others faced with crises similar to his own.

Rabbi Camille Angel, a young Jewish minister with a dynamic community on the Upper West Side of Manhattan, is not a right-to-die campaigner, and admits that her own feelings about the subject are not fully clear. In 1997, however, aware of its urgent social relevance, Angel chose the most solemn day of the Jewish calender, Yom Kippur, the Day of Atonement, to deliver a sermon on the importance of making living wills. On a day when God writes the Jewish people into the Book of Life or Death for the year to come, Angel chose to advise them of the need to be practically, as well as spirtually, prepared for what lay ahead. "More and more it is the law, not theology nor medicine, who is answering 'how' and 'when' we will die," Rabbi Angel told her congregation. "Each of us has a responsibility to choose for ourselves what we mean by living life. Today, I understand this religious imperative to mean that each of us is *required* to determine what treatment we want to get and what treatment we want to refuse."

Angel's congregation responded to her message by picking up hundreds of copies of the living wills that she had placed on a table outside the door. In the weeks that followed, many people told her they had filled them out. Only one congregant, Angel said, expressed profound disapproval of her sermon's content.

Jewish denominations, much like the various categories of Christians, differ widely on the issue of the right to die. Orthodox Jews, unsurprisingly, tend to oppose assisted dying, while the Reform and humanistic branches of Judaism respect the right of individuals to make their own decision. The differences have made for some fascinating debate among prominent Jewish leaders, both within the secular and the Jewish press. Rabbi Elliot Dorff, rector of the University of Judaism in Los Angeles, explained in the Jewish journal *Sh'ma* (September 20, 1996) that one reason for his opposition to assisted dying was that Jews should evaluate their lives "not solely in terms of the American values of pragmatism and hedonism, so that they are interested in living only if they can do things and enjoy life, but from the Jewish perspective which sees life as a divine gift with inherent worth regardless of the level of one's abilities."

In the same issue of the journal, psychiatrist Dr. Samuel C. Klagsbrun, executive medical director of Four Winds Hospital in Katonah, New York, countered that the reason he supports the practice is that, as a physician, "The guidance system I seek is trapped in a previous era, [and] I am left without a religious system because it has not kept pace with the problems current medical treatment has created. I cannot abandon my patients and I will do the best I can using my own judgment."

With his fierce commitment to medicine and his patients, it is no accident that Klagsbrun was one of three New York physicians who brought the issue of hastened death before the Second Circuit Court of Appeals in 1996, in the *Vacco v. Quill* case, the case that eventually made its way to the Supreme Court. But within the religious world, with which he is also very involved, Klagsbrun has not found much support among his peers. He says regretfully, "I feel very much alone in the position I've taken." He echoes Phifer and Falkowski when he adds, "Sadly, I do not believe that the courage is present in the religious community to struggle and grapple with these massively new and challenging dilemmas." It is a pessimistic appraisal.

Many bioethicists consider it is because of the failings of the religious community that their role at the deathbed has grown to fill the void. "The ethical community is stepping in to fill the breach, but we can't—it's not our job to provide emotional support," says bioethicist Arthur Caplan, director of the University of Pennsylvania's Center for Bioethics.

Their job, he says, demands greater distance: to act as society's moral arbiters, to provide conceptual, analytical critiques of the challenging new dilemmas that accompany modern medicine—among them, physician-assisted death. But even that is a struggle against a powerful tide: In forging a new set of moral answers to society's modern dilemmas, ethicists must battle a range of entrenched moral practices. In medicine, as everywhere else, old habits die hard. And physicians are particularly tenacious when fighting to maintain the status quo.

In his book *How We Die: Reflections of Life's Final Chapter,* Sherwin Nuland, clinical professor of surgery at Yale University, tells the story of a 92-year-old patient, Hazel Welch, who was rushed into the emergency room of Nuland's Boston hospital in serious condition, suffering from a perforated digestive tract. Nuland explained to her that she needed surgery, but Welch refused. She had lived long enough, she said. Now it was time to die.

Nevertheless, Nuland persuaded her to have the operation. It proved long and complicated, and although she survived, Welch scolded Nuland bitterly for having forced her to go through such a difficult ordeal. Had she known what it entailed, she said, she would have preferred to die. Two weeks later, back in her old-age home, she did die—of a stroke. Nuland, humbled by the experience, realized that "my treatment of Miss Welch was based not on her goals but on mine. . . . I pursued a form of futility that deprived her of the particular kind of hope she had longed for—that she could leave this world without interference when the opportunity arose. . . . Instead, she suffered the fate of so many of today's hospitalized dying, which is to be separated from reality by the very biotechnology and professional standards that are meant to return people to a meaningful life."

The incident Nuland describes happened in 1978, when he still felt the arrogance and invincibility of the young. But older and wiser as he may be, Nuland fears that very little has really changed. Faced with pressure from his peers, he admits, he might still behave in the same manner today.

"The code of the profession of surgery demands that no patient as salvageable as Miss Welch be allowed to die if a straightforward operation can save her," he writes. "We who would break that fundamental rule, no matter the humaneness of our motive, do so at our own peril. Viewed by a surgeon, mine was strictly a clinical decision, and ethics should not have been a consideration."

There is one difference, however, that Hazel Welch would find today: She would be able to call to her bedside an advocate, someone whose job it is to defend her right to self-determination. "Today, if you should land in a hospital, you may find that the single most important person assuring you the care you want may not hold a medical degree," says medical ethicist Nancy Neveloff Dubler in her book *Ethics on Call: A Medical Ethicist Shows How to Take Charge of Life-and-Death Choices.* "That person will hold the title of 'bioethicist,' 'clinical ethicist' or 'medical ethicist.'"

* * *

It is no coincidence that the field of bioethics is about the same age as the contemporary right-to-die movement: Both came into being prompted by the increasing complications of modern medicine, and the difficult questions raised by new biotechnologies. To begin with, the role of the ethicist was viewed as being essentially academic: thinking, writing, and postulating on issues from the safe distance of a university's philosophy department or an ivory-tower think tank. But in the past two decades, their work has expanded enormously in both theory and practice. Since the late 1970s and through the 1980s, ethicists have increasingly commonly taken up front-line positions in the trenches: working in health care centers and hospitals alongside the physicians and nurses, either alone or as part of a committee. Today, their work fulfills a recognized practical and spiritual service in most modern hospitals.

As part philosophers, part theologians, part lawyers, part social workers, ethicists have a difficult role to play. They tread an uneasy line between the pragmatic chaos of day-to-day medical care, with its inadequate amenities and resources, its inequitable provision for the rich and the uninsured, and its utopian ideals for the best possible outcomes for all. At best, they succeed in carving out real solutions in prickly situations. At worst, they erect defenses to protect their employers, justifying actions that may be morally or indeed ethically imperfect, in order to save their institutions from litigation and disrepute.

"Ethicists and philosophers are by trade troublemakers," says Margaret Battin, professor of philosophy at the College of Humanities, University of Utah. "They are interested in background assumptions and exploring issues that we once took for granted, but that when we look closer, are more complex than they seemed. We live in a culture of soundbites and easy answers. Ethicists don't settle for easy answers—they make things more complicated."

Things can't get much more complicated than at the end of life, when people are desperate to be spared suffering, pain, or, as they see it, the loss of dignity. Ethicists, better than most, know that the "good death" that so many of us envisage for ourselves—slipping away peacefully at the end of a long and productive life, surrounded by our loved ones—is increasingly becoming a fantasy. The harsher reality, according to the American Hospital Association, is that two out of three Americans will have what Dubler calls a "negotiated demise"—one in which the patient, his family and physicians must actively decide to stop or limit treatment to allow death to occur. "It has become very difficult to die in America," Dubler says. "It doesn't happen by accident, but by design."

All bioethicists can bring to mind difficult, emotional cases where they were forced to help a patient's design for him- or herself be realized. Connie Zuckerman, a medical ethicist with the United Hospital Fund in New York, recalls the case of a young man, an AIDS patient, who wanted his respirator turned off long before his physicians, and his family, were ready to let him go. It was Zuckerman's job to inform them all that the patient had the law of the land behind him, and the ethical right to make his stand. "It was hard work preparing everyone involved for that eventuality, but the patient himself was completely resolved," Zuckerman says. Similarly, Dubler, who works at the busy hospital complex of Montefiore Medical Center in New York, recalls trying to mediate in the case of an 85-year-old woman suffering from diabetes who preferred death to having a feeding tube inserted, and her daughter, who wanted to keep her alive. "There are no easy answers to these dilemmas," Dubler says. "They're not about finding happy endings."

A highly distressing example of a contemporary, end-of-life ethical drama was reported in the *Los Angeles Times* on February 10, 1997. It involved a 10-year-old who was declared "brain dead" by her hospital staff, and her fundamentalist Christian family, who refused to accept that definition of death. The anonymous bioethicist involved in the story explained that when the girl's family refused to let the hospital "unplug" her life-support machine, she eventually solved the dilemma by sending the girl's body home, still hooked up to the machine. When the girl's heart and other organs gave out 14 months later, the family finally accepted that the girl was dead.

Despite similar educational backgrounds and training, the bioethicists involved in the right-to-die debate have ended up with starkly divided views on the issue. For opponent Daniel Callahan, a cofounder of the Hastings Center for Bioethics in Westchester County, New York, assisted dying has posed frightening ethical questions that he has been trying to answer for almost 30 years. "As people have turned away from religion and elevated medicine as the supreme arbiter of our lives, we ask for medicine's sanction," Callahan has said. "Why? Because we need somebody in authority to say it is OK for us to do something that we know is reprehensible."

Jack Glaser, director of the Center for Health Care Ethics in Orange, California, is another fervent opponent. The center, started a dozen years ago by Sister of St. Joseph, Corrine Bayley, serves 250 California hospitals with educational materials on the subject of medical ethics, consultations, and the development of long-term schemes to alter hospitals' inherent attitudes toward death and care for the dying. Obviously, as a Catholic organization, the Center for Health Care Ethics inherently rejects the notion of physician-assisted dying. Yet Glaser insists that opposition stems from reasons far deeper than simple dogma. "I would hope that we would never form an opinion and stay with it if data proved us to be wrong," he says. "But if I ask whether our society would be better by empowering physicians to help people die, I can name any number of studies to show that the answer would be unequivocally "no.'"

At the other end of the spectrum, philosophers like Margaret Battin have campaigned for years to see assisted dying legalized. Battin believes that ethicists, like the population at large, form their opinions influenced by personal experience: that for those who have seen a loved one die badly, at close range, physician-assisted death is a welcome option, whereas those who see the issue only theoretically are less compelled to change the status quo.

"Part of what influences this may also be individuals' own assumptions about how they themselves are going to die," Battin goes on. "Often, those who are actively opposed to assisted death are those who think their own death will be caused by a heart attack or an accident. They don't imagine it will be cancer or ALS or any of the diseases with long, terminal courses. There's a watershed difference between people who feel they might find themselves in this kind of circumstance—probably because that's how their parents died—and those who are incapable of imagining it."

Battin feels the same sense of denial holds true for physicians. "Doctors always talk about their patients dying, never about their own death," she says. "On the other hand, doctors have access to drugs and they know what to do to help someone die. So they could all do this for a member of their family if they wanted that choice. Well, that's all that their patients want too."

Curiously, it's this disparity between the physicians, with their access to the means of hastened death, and their patients who are denied it, that is making Dubler, once a fierce opponent of assisted death, think twice about her position.

"I used to argue that physician-assisted dying would be a catastrophe for American society, given that we have no universal access to health care and no supports for those people who are too poor to gain access to it," she says. "But now it's clear to me that if I or any of my friends needed help with assisted suicide, we could get it—I have a number of colleagues who would give me a prescription. So by insisting that this not be made available to everyone, we're just adding one more burden to the life of the poor and the underprivileged and removing one more option. Arguments of compassion and consistency would insist on a way for individuals to end their lives as painlessly as possible. Whether the increasing inequities in American society can withstand this new set of powers, rights, and responsibilities without adding further indignity to our society is not yet clear."

Whatever their theoretical or public beliefs, it is almost inevitable that the realities of modern medicine—its impersonal haste, its less than impressive end-of-life care and inability to help patients address the spiritual aspects of their dying—will make our medical philosophers harbor personal feelings about the eventual determination of their own fates.

"Anyone who has witnessed these difficult deaths has got to feel sympathy for what advocates are fighting for," Zuckerman says. "But one can be very sympathetic to individual cases, yet still believe that it's too dangerous to base a public policy on them."

Caplan agrees that the policy implications of legalizing assisted dying are awesome, especially given the current inadequacy of this country's end-of-life services. "We do such a terrible job of providing people with terminal care and hospice care that I would have a lot of worries about how to implement assisted dying," Caplan says. Nevertheless, in more personal terms, this outspoken public critic concedes that he is not in principle opposed to the practice. His mellowing may in part be due to an experience that brought the dilemma of end-of-life care into his own family. Addressing a right to die conference in New York in November 1996, Caplan told the story of his father-in-law, who was dying in the hospital. During his father-in-law's entire stay, Caplan was amazed at the lack of personal attention and spiritual comfort offered by the medical staff who rushed in and out, always pressed for time. The most intimate communication he and his family had was with the repairman who came to fix the cable TV. The various medical professionals might argue that spiritual comfort is not their job. But there was no one else—other than the cable repairman—by the bedside.

CHAPTER 13

The Devil Is in
the Details
Navigating the
Nightmare Cases

We live in deeds, not years; in thoughts, not breaths.
—P. J. Bailey

When it comes to the new frontiers of medicine and bioethics, an important part of the experts' work is to project what could be done in worst-case scenarios:

What if a woman on fertility drugs becomes pregnant with eight fetuses and is vehemently opposed to aborting any of them, even though carrying all eight might endanger her life?

What if two patients were dying of liver disease, one a middle-aged alcoholic mother of three, the other a fit young man, and a liver becomes available for transplant? Which one should get the liver?

What if a genetic test can one day determine whether a fetus will grow up into an adult with a violent nature or a propensity for mental illness? Should the mother be given the option to abort it?

Such "what if" cases present a tough theoretical mental challenge. Physicians and medical ethicists thrash out hypothetical solutions at conferences, in think tanks, even on television shows. The extraordinary thing about life, of course, is that such cases, and some you could never even dream up, have occurred and will continue to occur.

So when these professionals worry that legalization of assisted dying may bring about errors or abuses, or provide the first layer of a slippery slope that will lead from voluntary suicide to voluntary euthanasia to involuntary euthanasia, or from physical illness to mental suffering, they may have genuine reasons to fear. In the Netherlands, where assisted suicide is not legal but physicians are not prosecuted for helping their patients to die, there have been acknowledged cases of abuse and mistakes, as well as a patient list that has included physically healthy patients, those who were mentally unstable, and in a few cases, even children euthanized without consent.

In the United States, even though the practice of assisted death is still illegal, there have also been a number of troublesome cases, shady and complex human dramas that embody the difficult issues under examination, and that illustrate how hard it is to make good legislation based on the vulnerabilities of human nature.

Among the most disturbing cases for all sides to decide are those involving patients with physical or mental conditions that are debilitating and unchanging, and that raise uncomfortable questions for society as a whole: What kind of "quality of life" do such patients really have, and who, if anyone, has a right to judge? What if there is no legally recognized health care proxy to represent the patient's wishes? And who decides when family members are divided about what they—and the muted patient—really want? One such case involves the beleaguered Klooster family of San Mateo, California. At the time of this writing, 2 years after it began, their sad dilemma has yet to be resolved.

Seventy-year-old Gerald Klooster, husband and father of five, was a robust and popular gynecologist when, in the early 1990s, he began suffering from the symptoms of Alzheimer's disease: memory loss, disorientation, and eventually, the failure to recognize friends and family members. Klooster, apparently, had watched his own mother die of Alzheimer's, and according to his wife of 44 years, Ruth, he did not want to end his life the same way. Ruth, claiming she was acting on her husband's instructions, contacted Jack Kevorkian.

But on hearing about the approach to Kevorkian, Chip Klooster, Gerald's oldest son, took his parents to court in an effort to win conservatorship of his father and to prevent his assisted suicide. Three of Klooster's children in California, who supported their brother Chip's views, also went to court, to try to win conservatorship there. But Ruth and the youngest son said they believed that suicide was a matter of personal choice, and that Gerald Klooster should be free to do with his life what he had told his wife he wanted.

The bitter battle split the family into two hostile camps. The judge at first awarded Chip custody of his father, and for several months, Klooster lived in Michigan with Chip's family. But in June 1996, Gerald Klooster was allowed to return home to California, to his wife.

One September night, some 3 months after returning home, Klooster arose in the night, went down to the kitchen, and took an overdose of sleeping pills, washed down with whiskey. According to Ruth, that is where she found him several hours later, comatose, lying on the floor. Ruth claimed he had made a suicide attempt despite her best efforts to take care of him. But Judge William McKinstry was suspicious; he said that Ruth Klooster "had waited too long before calling 911" and he was "troubled" by reports that she had interfered with the paramedics who had answered the emergency call.

Klooster spent several weeks in hospital and eventually made enough of a recovery to be sent home. But "home" where? Four of his children felt he would be unsafe if he went back to his wife. His wife insisted that was where he wanted to be. Again, the courts were called in to decide; Klooster's attorney argued that the old man had "the right to live where he wants and with whom he wants," namely, with his wife. But Judge McKinstry disagreed. He ordered Klooster to go live with his daughter, saying that, because of the presence of drugs and alcohol in their marital home, Ruth's care of her husband had been clearly inappropriate. He permitted Ruth to visit her husband only under supervision.

"I am simply struck and distressed by the circumstances [of this case]," the judge said. "It's tough to imagine this [was] an accident." McKinstry also made the controversial decision that Klooster's "do not resuscitate" request, included in his living will, should be destroyed—a decision that many right-to-die advocates immediately protested.

The Klooster case—which has already cost the family over $270,000—involves a number of the complexities that ethicists have almost certainly argued about in their theoretical cases: What if there is no legally recognized health care proxy to represent the patient's own wishes, and family members are divided about what they—and the silent patient—want? And which family member's decision takes precedence? The spouse's or the children's?

Even if relatives concur that before becoming unable to make her own decision clear, the patient had spoken of wanting to be helped to die, how can a physician be sure the patient had not been coerced into that decision, either because of money or because she didn't want to become a burden on her family?

And what if the patient has a chronic disease like Alzheimer's or ALS (amyotrophic lateral sclerosis, or Lou Gehrig's disease), where she is not "officially" terminally ill, but is clearly suffering and unhappy with the diminution of her life?

Although no law currently in effect or under consideration anywhere in the world asks for legalization of assisted suicide for chronically ill patients, there have already been cases in which such patients have been involved; for example, Janet Adkins, Dr. Kevorkian's first patient, who was in the early stages of Alzheimer's disease when she enlisted Kevorkian's services, and several subsequent patients, who had either Alzheimer's or ALS. (Supporters of broadening the category of patients eligible for assisted suicide add that chronic patients, with months or even years left to live, may be suffering more, and certainly for longer, than a terminal patient in the last days of life.)

But in an editorial in the *Journal of the American Medical Association* (January 16, 1991), James S. Goodwin, M.D., Mitchell Distinguished Professor of Geriatric Medicine at the University of Texas, and head of the Center on Aging, posed a provocative question about patients with chronic illnesses: "Whose suffering is being relieved?"

"My impression is that patients with Alzheimer's are no more or less happy than those with normal cognitive functioning," Goodwin writes. "But the families suffer terribly. There can be few agonies as great as witnessing the mental deterioration of a loved one. In many ways, the individual has died, but the mourning process cannot be resolved because he or she lives on. Add to this the physical burden of caregiving for a demented relative, and it should be very clear who is suffering. It should also be clear who are the recipients of mercy in the mercy killing of an Alzheimer's patient. What do we hear over and over from the interviews, the docudramas, the analyses? 'I couldn't stand to see her suffer.' Mercy killing, like all killing, is the ultimate selfish act."

*   *   *

Of the many cases involving chronic illness that have grabbed public attention over the past few years, none has contained so many ambiguities of motivation and intent as that involving George Delury, the 63-year-old New Yorker who helped his 52-year-old wife, Myrna Lebov, to end her life in July 1995. At the time of her death, Lebov had been suffering from multiple sclerosis for more than 20 years and Delury maintained that her quality of life had declined to such a degree that she no longer wanted to live. But Lebov's sister, Beverly Sloane, insisted that Delury had coerced her into her decision, and a diary that Delury had been keeping in the months before her death revealed how frustrated he was by her deteriorating condition.

Did Delury help his wife to die as a true act of mercy, or was this mercy killing, as Goodwin suggests, the ultimate selfish act? Was it, in fact, a mercy killing at all? In New York City, where Delury lives, an enthralled local media documented every twist and turn of the case. Delury, and every right-to-die "expert" on the East Coast, pro and con, was asked for their interpretation. The wide disparity of responses was proof enough of the complexities involved in this troubling and haunting case.

It was Delury himself who called the police early on the morning of July 4, 1995, to tell them that he had just helped his ailing wife to take a lethal overdose of her antidepressant medication, Elavil. The night before, Delury said, the two had eaten a special meal of chicken and wine together that he had gone out to buy. After dinner, he had stirred the contents of her capsules, which he had been stockpiling, into a mixture of water and honey and had brought them to her in two cups, with a straw to help her drink. Lebov drank the potion with fixed determination and shortly after swallowing it, she slipped into a deep sleep, and several hours later, took her final breath.

Delury, after keeping watch for some hours at Myrna's bedside, dropped off to sleep and woke up at around 5:30 AM to find her dead. He called the police shortly after 6, and when they offered him instructions in CPR, he refused them, saying that he had helped her to die. As a result of this confession, Delury was taken into custody later that day and charged with second-degree manslaughter, a felony that carries with it a maximum term of 5 to 15 years in jail. After a night in a cell, Delury was released on bail on his own recognizance.

Initially, the press as a whole treated the story as a standard "mercy killing" of a suffering woman by her loyal husband. Reporters descended on Delury and Lebov's Upper West Side home and interviewed doormen and neighbors about the devoted couple who had been together for 22 years. Neighbors spoke of how lately they had stopped seeing her maneuvering her way courageously around the neighborhood in her electric wheelchair, and how word was that her condition had deteriorated considerably within recent months. Others remembered how happy the two had been years ago, but how depressed and haggard Delury had come to look. The consensus was that this devoted husband had worn himself out in caring for his rapidly ailing wife. He had done the humane and self-sacrificing thing: He had helped to put her out of her misery. Right-to-die advocates flocked to Delury's side with offers of counsel and financial aid. "I didn't do this to become anyone's poster boy," Delury said shortly after the event. But it was obviously gratifying to be hailed—at least by some—as a kind of hero.

But when extracts from the diary he was keeping were made public, the press coverage—and Delury's image— quickly changed. Delury had started the diary just a few months before Lebov's death, and he freely handed it to the police as soon as they arrived at his home. He seemed oblivious of its incriminating phrases and tone. "You are sucking the life out of me like a vampire and nobody cares," one entry read. Another described Lebov as living a "meat loaf life." He frequently refers to her as a "burden," and admitted later that he had even, on occasion, called her a burden to her face.

In light of Delury's journal entries and accusations by Lebov's sister, Beverly Sloane, that Delury had pressured her into ending her life, New York's district attorney, Robert Morgenthau, made it clear that he was seriously considering prosecuting the case as an assisted murder. As such, Delury stood to receive a 15-year prison sentence and legal fees that he feared he would never be able to repay. In the end, the district attorney's office accepted a plea bargain and settled for a 6-month prison term. Delury became the first American ever to serve a sentence for assisting in the death of a loved one.

When I first met Delury, shortly after Lebov's death on a sweltering summer afternoon, he spoke to me sitting crumpled in Myrna's wheelchair in the couple's bedroom among the mementos of their former life—a box of adult diapers, the motorized wheelchair, a white noticeboard on which Delury would write for her the day's date and list of activities. He spoke of her with great love and admiration, and frequently broke down in tears while talking of her. He recalled for me their meeting in 1968 at the research firm where they both were working, his proposal of marriage to her (he was already divorced from a first wife), which she initially turned down, and the subsequent few months when they decided not to see one another. He told me how, by the time he called her again, she spoke of having developed some ominous symptoms: dizziness and disorientation, numbness and tingling in her limbs. From her descriptions, Delury suspected that she was suffering from multiple sclerosis, a diagnosis her physician confirmed shortly afterwards. He proposed to her again, and this time, she accepted.

There were a number of good years where the couple worked productively—he as a freelance editor, she as a writer—and where Lebov's condition remained reasonably stable. I asked him to show me a picture of her when she was well, and he eagerly brought out a photograph album of the two of them in earlier, healthier times—on vacation in Ireland and Israel, walking in stony landscapes, wading in the sea.

But in 1989, Lebov's condition began to deteriorate quickly. She tired easily and soon found walking too hard, relying on a wheelchair to go out. One night in 1991, she fell in the bedroom and never walked again. Slowly, writing, reading, washing, and dressing herself—everything became too difficult to do alone. For Delury, the most upsetting signs were that his once keenly intellectual companion was having trouble following a conversation or reading a book.

"How helpless I have become!" she wrote to her sister, Beverly Sloane, who lived in California. "I can't do much for myself anymore. Can't cut my food, touch-type, wipe my ass, turn over in bed, travel by myself, etc. etc. Translation: No freedom. I've been trapped in my life with no escape—except suicide."

Lebov and Delury had talked about suicide as an option since mid-1991. In 1993, she had written to a close friend that suicide was "the only honorable course of action." By mid-1995, both knew that the time was drawing nearer. She spoke to her sister, Beverly, about her decision, as well as to Beverly's daughter, Alison, who lived near her aunt in Manhattan and who was a regular visitor. Her relatives say they worked hard to dissuade Lebov from doing anything drastic. They claim to have arranged therapy sessions, checked on her frequently, and offered her money to help ease the financial difficulties that were a constant in Delury and Lebov's life. (Delury insists that Beverly was never really there for her sister; that Myrna carefully vetted what she told her because Beverly "didn't really want to know," and that one reason she decided to commit suicide when she did was that she was bitterly disappointed with her sister's passivity toward her.)

Whatever the truth, Beverly and Alison have both said that just days before her death, Lebov had spoken to them about her renewed desire to live. She even made plans with Alison to attend a play in Central Park the following week. But Delury says she often spoke that way when she entered a "euphoric" phase. Days later, when her mood turned to depression again, she would have no recall of those upbeat conversations.

It was the constant changing of her state of mind, Delury said, that became increasingly hard to take. "Unless people can see the process hour by hour, it's hard to understand how terrible that is," he said. "God and the Devil are in the details."

By now, the New York newspapers had made up their minds where they stood on this story. *New York Newsday* and the weekly *Jewish Forward* made their disapproval patently clear.

"Although Mr. Delury has suggested he cared for his ailing wife as a labor of love, in the course of several conversations with the Forward he made it clear it was labor, and unrewarded labor, at that," the weekly's reporter wrote. A large, three-page feature in *Newsday* suggested Delury acted out of arrogance and self-interest, an accusation that clearly upset him. "If the people who accused me of this knew me, I'd feel terrible, I'd really have to take it to heart," he said.

But the *New York Times,* although mildly critical of Delury himself, took another approach to the issue. In both an editorial and an opinion piece submitted by the American Suicide Foundation's Herbert Hendin, the *Times* stressed the importance of recognizing the pressures that are placed on the caregivers of severely ill patients. Delury made much of this point in the weeks after the event, insisting over and over that he had been overextended and burnt-out by caring for Lebov, and that no one had been concerned about *his* welfare—only hers.

"Mr. Delury's despair over the unrelieved drudgery of attending to his wife's bodily functions and emotional needs reflects a widespread desperation among the seriously (but not necessarily terminally) ill and their families," Hendin wrote. "It is time to provide a solution—affordable home care—that does not pit patients and families against each other."

The *Times* suggested that by making physician-assisted death available in such cases, "many people caught in such terrible pressures would turn to the medical profession for help."

Some 3 years after Myrna Lebov's death, George Delury has a new life. He served 4 months of his 6-month prison sentence in a minimum-security prison in Queens, New York (he got 2 months off for good behavior) and while inside, he wrote a book about what had happened, *But What If She Wants to Die?* In it, Delury made the confession, never previously disclosed, that he had helped Myrna to die by putting a plastic bag over her head. He explained that although she had been rendered comatose by the drug overdose, she was still breathing regularly as dawn approached. Afraid that a health aide would arrive before she was dead and would try to revive her, Delury described how he pulled two plastic bags over her head and secured them in place with a ribbon. Lebov's breathing ceased shortly after.

This revelation caused widely expressed shock and disgust. Once again, *New York Newsday* ran the story, illustrated by a large, somber picture of Delury, over its entire front page, with the headline " 'Suicide' by Suffocation." The Manhattan attorney general said regretfully that Delury could not be retried for his role in her death, as that would constitute double jeopardy. However, Lebov's sister, Beverly Sloane, immediately filed a civil suit for wrongful death. The case is still underway, along with a state investigation as to whether the revenues from Delury's book, at present being kept in an escrow account by his publishers, can be forfeited under the so-called Son of Sam law that bars criminals from profiting from their crimes.

Delury defended his use of the plastic bag as simply "an ugly and horrific moral necessity" brought about by "laws no longer congruent with the modern medical environment. I would be a strange assistant indeed," he said, "if, having begun, I changed my mind in the middle of the process and opened the possibility of her resuscitation—against her will." However, he realizes that, for some people, the concept of using a plastic bag to help someone die elicits a visceral sense of horror that can't be intellectualized away. "Some people just couldn't do it," he acknowledges. "I understand that."

As he awaits the outcome of the lawsuit, Delury is trying to rebuild his life. He has plans to write another book and has begun teaching literacy classes a couple of evenings a week. He has also become a sometime counselor for the dying. Some people have contacted him via the Hemlock Society, of which he is an active member, others have searched him out independently. One of the women who sought his counsel ended up becoming a patient of Kevorkian's. At her request, Delury accompanied her on her one-way journey to Michigan. He returned to New York after her death, alone.

It would be presumptuous to speculate on how Delury feels about his life since his wife's death, whether knowing what he does now, he would be prepared to do it all again. He says he has no regrets about what has happened, but it has obviously had an enormous cost. Some friends have dropped him, he says, as has one of his main employers. Uncomfortable with the reactions of various members of his congregation, he has even stopped attending his synagogue on a regular basis. His religious beliefs, as well as his frequent visits to the temple, had always been a source of comfort, he once told me. I see him sometimes on the streets of the Upper West Side. He is always alone.

For us, the public, the Delury case has raised a number of enduring questions: about the physical and mental demands involved in caring long-term for the severely ill, about the role depression may play in the lives of family members as well as patients, and about the questionable motivations involved in relatives helping their loved ones end their lives. Finally, are there lessons in this case to help us better understand what happens to those who open up the Pandora's box of assisted suicide?

What Delury's situation may have shed most light on is the profound range of emotions that death can evoke. On one level, he admits, he wanted Lebov's death, but now he claims he is bereft by her loss. "While my life is in some ways better, in other ways it's so disastrously worse that I'll never recover," he says. "The lack of her is just. . . ." His words peter out. Beverly Sloane's life is also diminished, she claims, along with that of her husband and daughter, Alison. She too says she will never recover from the manner of her sister's death. But it has given her a new direction in her life: Still bitter toward Delury and haunted by her sister's end, she is now working on a project involving the ethics surrounding assisted suicide.

Time and again, the media wrestled to find an easy way to interpret Delury's actions: Was he a devoted husband, a selfish tyrant, or a kind of naif: a man who was so devoid of guile that he simply did not realize how incriminating it would be to expose the innermost thoughts he recorded in his journal, and the actions he took that he wrote of in his book? Perhaps the most difficult answer to accept is that maybe Delury was all three. And that, in publishing his ignoble feelings as well as his pain, Delury gave voice to a dark side of human nature that many of us may share but are too afraid of in ourselves to articulate. How many of us have wished that the prolonged suffering of a loved one would end? How many of us have thought how much easier life would be without having to care for a needy or dependent relative? How many of us have fantasized about helping that loved one to die? And how big is the step between thought and action? Delury was not afraid to expose his dark urges—even though they were ignoble ones. "My diary is a warts-and-all exposure of my thoughts and feelings at the time," he says. "I didn't want to emerge looking like a saint or a villain, so it's all there. There are no saints or sinners in this, whatever anyone wants to say. This is simply a tragedy of ordinary people."

Postscript

In the months since I began writing this book, one question has come up over and over again: Isn't it depressing to write about death? The answer is no, not depressing. It has been sometimes shocking, sometimes heart-wrenching, sometimes inspirational, and always thought-provoking. I have thought a great deal, not just about the rights and wrongs of assisted dying, but about what it means to die: the important visceral place death occupies in our psyche throughout our lifetime, and the journey that our physical dying involves, from the earliest acknowledgment of what is happening to the final leave-taking.

As someone who grew up with an impression of death as both unnatural and unbearable, I have had a great deal to learn about overcoming fear and understanding dying as something that could be peaceful and even healing. Unconsciously, I think I hoped that researching this book would help me at least start to glimpse some of these possibilities.

Ironically, the lesson I was striving to learn intellectually was finally taught to me by Aunty. It was as I sat by her bedside, watching her life slowly come to a close, that I came to see how, under certain circumstances, the prolongation of life can be a curse, and death can truly be a blessing and a release.

It took Aunty a year and a half to die after her amputation. It was a heartbreaking time during which she lost not only her physical independence and the ability to do the things she loved—traveling, going to parks, and cooking meals for her family—but ultimately also her will to live.

From the time she was admitted to hospital after her fall, she was never able to return to her home again; she was moved from the hospital to a long-term rehabilitation unit, and after 7 months there, to an old-age home. Although she worked hard at the rehab hospital to learn to use a prosthetic leg, she didn't have enough upper-body strength to manage it. Confined to a wheelchair, she could no longer look after herself and felt demeaned and appalled every time she had to summon a nurse to take her to the bathroom.

Among my many trips to London to see her, the saddest was to dismantle her apartment after she conceded she would never be able to return there. For most people, the miserable task of dispersing the prized possessions of a lifetime takes place after their death, when they are no longer around to feel the loss. Aunty lived to experience that sorrow. Almost all of her many belongings had to be sold or given away, as there was no way that most of them would fit into her small room in the old-age home.

She moved into the home in early summer, and for a few months, she could sit in the garden with her visitors, enjoying the heat of an unusually sultry English summer. But as the season waned and autumn turned to winter, the parameters of her world shrunk inward, bound by the small walls of her room. It was too cold to go out, and sitting in the communal living room among those she called "the shriekers and the shakers" depressed her even more. Her hearing, always bad, deteriorated so much that she could no longer use the telephone; visitors had to shout directly into her ear. From New York, all I could do was fax weekly letters to her. To find out how she was doing, I had to telephone her nurses: It was a task I came to dread more and more.

So Aunty would sit gazing out of her window for days on end, her mood alternating between blunt depression and a frantic, lashing rage about how wretched her life had become. By Christmastime, she was telling everyone who would listen that she wanted to die. She begged her nurses and her physician to help her. Of course, they said they couldn't. Indeed, even if assisted dying were legal, Aunty would not have been a candidate. She had not been diagnosed with a terminal illness or as having only 6 months to live, even though at 91, and with deteriorating general health, she was clearly on a downward path. All of her friends agreed that her predicament was pitiful, and that her suffering was great. But there was nothing to be done for her. Ironically, although she had virtually stopped eating, she dutifully continued to take her numerous daily medications. I asked her why she bothered, and she hedged the question, implying that she was afraid not to. I'm still not sure whether she was afraid to disobey, or afraid to play an active role in precipitating her death. What she wanted, she explained to me, was for death to come like a thunderbolt, to take her, quickly and painlessly, for life simply to stop.

In January 1998, it finally did. Happily, I was with her at the time. I had come to see her for a few days, aware that her physical condition had deteriorated, but unprepared for a crisis. On our first day together, she seemed depressed, but physically stable. Yet when I arrived the following morning, I found her gasping for air. Her final illness, a serious chest infection that caused her lung to collapse, lasted 4 days. She spent the final two of them in the hospital, two small tubes filtering oxygen into her rasping chest, and an intravenous drip administering a mixture of drugs into her bloodstream to ease her general discomfort. For most of the time, she was unconscious. On the final day, I was sitting at her bedside when her eyelids flickered open and she drew her last quiet gasps, and became suddenly still. In the end, it looked so easy.

But the suffering Aunty endured through her final traumatic 18 months haunts me still. Although she was never in great pain, I am convinced that her psychological and existential torment were as unbearable as any physical suffering could be. She told me that had she known what her life would be like after the amputation, she would never have gone ahead with it. But I wonder: When she was faced with that decision, she was not ready to die; she couldn't imagine how diminished her life would become—what it would mean when stripped of all of the activities she prized. How difficult it must be for anyone to choose death when, up until that point, they have only experienced life under normal circumstances. After all, the survival instinct is powerful indeed: I saw for myself how tenaciously Aunty clung to hope, even at age 90; the hope of walking again, and when that failed, the hope that she could use an electric wheelchair to gain some kind of freedom. She didn't give up hope for a very long time.

When she did, she was ready: ready to die, prepared and unafraid. And by being with her during those last days, I saw how sometimes, dying is not tragic and terrible, but simply an inevitable end, a relief and a release. I had never experienced a death like that before: a quiet, natural culmination of a long life fully lived. Doing so freed me from a lifelong fear of my own—the fear that dying is always something cruel and traumatic. This is also a fear from which supporters of assisted dying are trying to free themselves when they ask for help with their deaths.

As all of the experiences discussed in this book have revealed, dying in the modern world is often hard: protracted, painful, and existentially lonely—a journey taken without adequate guides. The right-to-die movement has developed as a response to this—as a desperate call to make things better, by providing the quick, lethal dose of medicine that, for many, seems preferable to the dreadful suffering and isolation of a slow death.

All of us—those who support the right-to-die cause and its opponents too—owe a great deal to this movement. It has, for the first time in our terrified culture, opened up the debate and faced down the taboos. In less than 20 years, the debate has extended far beyond talk. As a result of Dr. Kevorkian, Derek Humphry's *Final Exit,* the Oregon Death with Dignity Act, and the desperate acts of hundreds of individuals—some secret, some not—America's medical, ethical, and religious communities have begun to glimpse what is wrong with our society's way of death and how we need to improve it.

One sign of hope is the spread of the hospice movement, one of the most successful medical developments of the last quarter-century. For a combination of reasons—from restrictions in Medicare to a still-widespread misunderstanding that hospices are for patients who have "given up"—only 14 percent of Americans, an estimated 400,000 a year, avail themselves of hospice care. Those who do find a sophisticated system of palliative, or comfort, care, where the emphasis is not on trying to cure the incurable, but rather on making the dying patient peaceful and comfortable. In hospices, physicians prescribe painkilling drugs without fear of causing addiction, and reject high-tech interventions in favor of a hands-on, humanistic approach that supports the patient's spiritual and emotional needs.

It will be interesting to discover whether this revolutionary form of end-of-life care can coexist with the demand for assisted dying. If patients are offered an early way out, will anyone accept the notion of being made comfortable while they wait for death to arrive naturally? If hospices know that a hastened death is what a patient plans, will they still be prepared to take the patient in? "If they do, it will be fundamental change in hospice policy," says ethicist Caplan. "I believe it will bring the concept of hospice as we know it to an end."

In the meantime, however, in their attempts to improve end-of-life care, a number of orthodox health care organizations have been adopting aspects of hospice philosophy. New York's United Hospital Fund has launched a project to improve palliative care in 12 New York City hospitals. The Robert Wood Johnson Foundation has launched Last Acts, a national initiative involving some 70 health care organizations, also designed to improve the conditions of the dying. Among its goals: upgrading medical students' training and ensuring that health-insurance plans cover end-of-life care services, such as hospice and pain management. Meanwhile, a newly formed organization, Americans for Better Care of the Dying (ABCD), plans to lobby for changes, both in government and in society.

Project on Death in America has similarly ambitious objectives. Financed with $15 million by the billionaire philanthropist George Soros, the project was born in 1994 when he became aware of the harm that is caused by society's refusal to confront the realities of dying. At its launch, Soros said he wanted to "promote a better understanding of the experiences of dying and bereavement and by doing so transform the culture surrounding death." It is the work of a lifetime.

Yet, with small steps forward, the journey has begun, and the questions that it raises are profound. What will dying be like in the future? Will we ever have methods of alleviating pain so sophisticated as to promise everyone a comfortable death? Will we all eventually face the end in a hospice, with our loved ones beside us, or at home with daily life going on all around? Will our physicians help us if we need it? And if not physicians, will the job be done by a nurse, or a specially qualified "euthanasia specialist"—the "obitiatrist" of Dr. Kevorkian's brave new world?

The implications of all of these prospects are far-reaching. Many fear they will take us into territory where we don't belong. But the twentieth century has witnessed achievements by men and women that have already stretched the bounds of human understanding. We have explored the galaxies, split the atom, and cloned a mammal. We are deep into God's terrain, and now there can be no turning back. We're all in it together—to the death.

Bibliography

Angell, Marcia. "Euthanasia in the Netherlands: Good News or Bad?" *New England Journal of Medicine* 355 (Nov. 1996).

Anonymous. "It's Over, Debbie." *Journal of the American Medical Association* 259, no. 2 (Jan. 1988).

"Australians Provide Deliverance on the Internet." *The Lancet Online* 348, no. 9037 (Nov. 1996).

Betzold, Michael. "The Selling of Doctor Death." *The New Republic* (May 26, 1997).

Breitbach, W., Rosenfeld, S., et al. "The Undertreatment of Pain in Ambulatory AIDS Patients." *Pain* 65 (1996).

Burnell, George M., M.D. *Final Choices: To Live or to Die in an Age of Medical Technology.* New York: Plenum Press, 1993.

Casimir, Jon. Netwatch. Sitings. *The Age.* Melbourne (Jan. 2, 1997).

Conwell and Caine. "Rational Suicide and the Right to Die: Reality and Myth." *New England Journal of Medicine* 325 (1991).

Delury, George E. *But What If She Wants to Die?* Secaucus, NJ: Birch Lane Press, Carol Publishing Group, 1997.

Dubler, Nancy Neveloff and David Nimmons. *Ethics on Call: A Medical Ethicist Shows How to Take Charge of Life-and-Death Choices.* New York: Harmony Books, 1982.

Fadiman, Anne. "Death News: Requiem for the Hemlock Quarterly." *Harpers* 288, no. 1727 (April 1994).

Goodwin, James S. "Mercy Killing: Mercy for Whom?" *Journal of the American Medical Association* 265, no. 3 (Jan. 1991).

Hendin, Herbert. "Dying of Resentment." *New York Times* (March 21, 1996).

———. *Seduced by Death: Doctors, Patients, and the Dutch Cure.* New York: W.W. Norton, 1997.

Hentoff, Nat. "The Poster Doctor for Euthanasia." *Village Voice* (Feb. 11, 1997).

Hill T. Patrick and David Shirley. *A Good Death: Taking More Control at the End of Your Life.* Reading, MA: Addison–Wesley, 1992.

Hoefler, James M. with Brian E. Kamoie. *Deathright: Culture, Medicine, Politics, and the Right to Die.* Boulder, CO: Westview Press, 1994.

Humphry, Derek. *Final Exit.* Secaucus, NJ: Hemlock Society, 1991.

———. *Let Me Die Before I Wake: Hemlock's Book of Self-Deliverance for the Dying.* New York: Dell, 1992.

———. "What's in a Word?" *ERGO! Euthanasia Research and Guidance Organization* (1993).

Humphry, Derek and Ann Wickett. *Jean's Way.* New York: Quarter Books, 1978.

———. *The Right to Die.* New York: Harper and Row, 1986.

James, Sheryl. "For the Defense of Dr. Death." *Los Angeles Times Magazine* (Nov. 10, 1996).

Jerome, Richard, *et al.* "Post Mortem." *People* (Sept. 16, 1996).

Kaplan, Kalman J., Ph.D. and Janelle DeWitt. "Kevorkian's List: Gender Bias or What?" *American Association of Suicidology, News Link* 22, no. 3 (Fall 1996).

Kevorkian, Dr. Jack. *Prescription: Medicine, The Goodness of Planned Death.* Buffalo, NY: Prometheus Books, 1991.

Klagsbrun, Samuel C. "Physician Assisted Suicide." *Sh'ma: The National Jewish Center for Learning and Leadership* (Sept. 20, 1996).

Lagnado, Lucette. "DA Stepping Up Inquiry in Death of Myrna Lebov." *The Forward* (Sept. 21, 1995).

Lenox, William G. "Should They Live?" *American Scholar* no. 454 (1938).

Lewin, Tamar. "Suits Accuse Medical Community of Ignoring 'Right to Die' Orders." *New York Times* (June 2, 1996).

Lynn, Joanne, *et al.* "The Study to Understand Prognoses and Preferences for Outcomes and Risks of Treatment (SUPPORT)." *Annals of Internal Medicine* 16 (Jan. 1997).

MacDonald, W. et al. "Ohio Death and Dying Survey." Ohio State University (1994).

McCrystal, Cal. "Ann Humphry's Final Exit." *Vanity Fair* (Jan. 1992).

Moreno, Jonathan D., ed. *Arguing Euthanasia: The Controversy Over Mercy Killing, Assisted Suicide, and the "Right to Die."* New York: Touchstone Books, 1995.

Nuland, Sherwin B. *How We Die: Reflections of Life's Final Chapter.* New York: Alfred A. Knopf, 1994.

Ogden, Russell. *Euthanasia, Assisted Suicide, and AIDS.* New Westminster, B.C.: Peroglyphics, 1994.

Pappas, Demetra M. "Recent Historical Perspectives Regarding Medical Euthanasia and Physician Assisted Suicide." *British Medical Bulletin* 52, no. 2 (1996).

Pernick, Martin, *The Black Stork: Eugenics and the Death of*

'Defective' Babies in American Medicine and Motion Pictures since 1915. London: Oxford University Press, 1996.

Perron, Marshall. "How the First Euthanasia Law Was Passed." *World Right-to-Die Newsletter* no. 29 (Nov. 1996).

Prip, William and Anna Moretti. "Compliance: The Missing Component in Patient Autonomy Laws." *Choice in Dying* (Spring 1996).

Quill, Timothy E., M.D. "Death and Dignity: A Case of Individualized Decision Making." *New England Journal of Medicine* (March 7, 1991).

————. *Death and Dignity: Making Choices and Taking Charge.* New York: W.W. Norton, 1993.

Quill, Timothy E. and Betty Rollin. "Dr. Kevorkian Runs Wild." *New York Times* (Aug. 29, 1996).

Rollin, Betty. *Last Wish.* New York: Simon & Schuster, 1985.

Rosenbaum, Ron. "Angel of Death: The Trial of the Suicide Doctor." *Vanity Fair* (May 1991).

Ruwart, Mary with Sue Woodman. "To Die with Dignity." *McCalls* (Feb. 1994).

Shavelson, Lonnie. *A Chosen Death: The Dying Confront Assisted Suicide.* New York: Simon and Schuster, 1995.

Siegel, Barry. "A Debate Over Life After Death." *Los Angeles Times* (Feb. 10, 1997).

Slome, Lee R., Thomas F. Mitchell, Edwin Charlebois, *et al.* "Physician-Assisted Suicide and Patients with Human Immunodeficiency Virus Disease." *New England Journal of Medicine* 336 (Feb. 1997).

Solomon, M., *et al.* "Professional Views of Life-Sustaining Treatments." *American Journal of Public Health* 83 (1993).

SUPPORT Principal Investigators. "A Controlled Trial to Improve Care for Seriously Ill Hospitalized Patients: The Study to Understand Prognoses and Preferences for Outcomes and Risks of Treatment (SUPPORT)." *Journal of the American Medical Association* 274, no. 20 (Nov. 22–29, 1995).

Treneman, Ann. "Twenty-first Century Way of Death?" *Independent on Sunday* (Sept. 29, 1996).

Voboril, Maril. "His Wife Killed Herself. He Helped." *New York Newsday* (Jan. 16, 1996).

Webb, Marilyn. *The Good Death.* New York: Bantam Books, 1977.

Werth, James, Jr., Ph.D. *Rational Suicide? Implications for Mental Health Professionals.* London: Taylor and Francis, 1996.

Wickett, Ann. *Double Exit.* Secaucus, NJ: Hemlock Society, 1989.

Wilkes, Paul. "The Case Against Doctor Assisted Suicide." *New York Times Magazine* (July 21, 1996)

Acknowledgments

There are so many people to acknowledge for their valuable contributions in helping me write this book.

First, my heartfelt thanks to all of the dozens of people who talked to me so openly about their work, their philosophy, and their experiences. I am especially grateful to those who, despite great sadness and suffering, decided to share their personal stories with me—either publicly or confidentially—for the sake of this book.

For help with research, my grateful thanks to Christopher Brimer, Susan Volchok, Pieter de Hoop, Lucie Kaye, the ever-vigilant Leon Arden, John Hofsess, Derek Humphry for his generosity with two decades' worth of accumulated data, and Steven A. Newman, professor of law at New York Law

School. My appreciation also to Laura Manske, the friend and editor who gave me the assignment that led to this book.

Thanks too to Danielle Maggio, Margarita Danielian, and James Armstrong for their editorial skills, and to my editor at Plenum Publishing, Erika Goldman, for more than she can realize.

There are a number of people to whom I owe an especially large debt of gratitude: Sarah Dunant, for her boundless friendship and tireless mind; Thea Stone, for her extraordinary wisdom and support; my dear friend Frances Hill, for going out of her way for me; and Katherine Sands, my agent, for nurturing and encouraging this project—and me—every step of the way. Katherine has been everything, and much more, that an agent should be.

My greatest appreciation goes to Helen Rogan for her tremendous talent and her friendship, both so warmly given. I shall be ever grateful for her great generosity of spirit.

Finally, thanks and love to my glorious children, Sophie and Jake, for being motherless with such good grace for many months, and to Michael Mathewson, who makes everything possible.

Index